W9-DDQ-463

AMERICAN JEWRY
AND
CONSERVATIVE POLITICS

A New Direction

Alan J. Steinberg

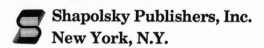
Shapolsky Publishers, Inc.
New York, N.Y.

Copyright © 1988 by Alan J. Steinberg

All rights reserved under International and Pan American
Copyright Conventions. Published and printed in the U.S.A. by
Shapolsky Publishers, Inc. No parts of this book may be used or
reproduced in any manner whatsoever without written
permission of Shapolsky Publishers, Inc., except in the case of
brief quotations embodied in critical articles or reviews.

For any additional information, contact:
Shapolsky Publishers, Inc.
136 West 22nd Street, NY, NY 10011

First Edition

1 2 3 4 5 6 7 8 9 10

Library of Congress Cataloging in Publication Data

Steinberg, Alan J., 1949 -

American Jewry and conservative politics: a new direction

1. Jews—United States—Politics and Government.
2. Conservatism—United States. 3. United States—Politics and
Government—1945. 4. United States—Ethnic relations.
I. Title.

E184.J5S79 1988   305.8'924'073—dc19   88-24027

ISBN 0-933503-86-5

Printed in the United States of America

Dedication

To my late grandparents, Archie Steinberg, Louis Miller, and Bessie Perr Miller, who came to America from lands of persecution and dedicated their lives to a better life for their descendants, and to my late grandmother, Rose Steinberg, whose long life and unwavering dedication to her family and the Jewish way of life still serve as an inspiration and hope to her children, grandchildren and great-grandchildren.

To my parents, Melvin and Harriet Steinberg, whose greatest gift to their children was our Jewish heritage.

To Rabbi Albert L. Lewis and Cantor Mordecai Fuchs of Temple Beth Sholom, Haddon Heights, New Jersey, who more than anyone else have taught me the joys and meaning of the Jewish way of life.

To my son, Neil, who has taught me the real meaning of love and whose generation will determine the future of American Jewry.

Table of Contents

About the Author

Alan J. Steinberg is an attorney residing in northern New Jersey. Born in Pittsburgh, Pennsylvania in 1949, he attended Northwestern University in Evanston, Illinois and was graduated with honors in political science. After receiving his law degree at the University of Wisconsin in 1974, he then served three years as Lieutenant in the United States Navy Judge Advocate General's Corps. Since returning to civilian life in May, 1977, he has served as an attorney in both private and corporate law practice. He has been extremely active in conservative and Republican political circles. Mr. Steinberg served as an official surrogate speaker for Ronald Reagan's 1980 and 1984 Presidential campaigns. He has also written a number of editorial columns appearing in New Jersey newspapers and has appeared as a guest on various Philadelphia radio shows.

In addition to his career in law and politics, Mr. Steinberg has also served as a professional cantor for Conservative synagogues.

Mr. Steinberg has been extremely active in Jewish community affairs, serving on the Board of Directors of Temple Beth Sholom, Haddon Heights, New Jersey and as president of Hashomer Lodge B'nai B'rith, Cherry Hill, New Jersey. He is the father of a son, Neil, 8.

Introduction: A Jewish Conservative's Odyssey

"Alan, what's a nice Jewish boy like you doing as a conservative Republican?"

During the past ten years, I have been asked this question numerous times by fellow members of my synagogue, volunteers in Jewish organizations, and even relatives. What strikes me is the way the question is posed. It is as if my conservative political philosophy was somehow at variance with my diligent observance of Jewish custom, tradition, and law.

This is a book that is much more than an answer to this question. My central thesis is that post-1960 political liberalism is not only detrimental to the future of American society but, in fact, poses an even greater threat to the survival and welfare of American Jewry and America's relationship with the State of Israel.

In his landmark book, *Jews and American Politics*, published in 1974, the distinguished writer, Stephen D. Isaacs, asserts that the notion that Jews are liberal voters is in fact a myth. He cogently sets forth data asserting that the main motivation of Jewish voters is fear for their security, based upon the history of persecution of Jews in the Diaspora. Isaacs argues that Jews have tended to vote for liberal candidates because they felt that they have far less to fear from them than their conservative opponents.

I believe that there is a strong element of validity in Mr. Isaac's argument. I write this book in the wake of a 1984 campaign in which many Jews voted for Walter Mondale over Ronald Reagan for President because they felt they had more to fear from the

Reverend Jerry Falwell in the Republican camp than the Democrat Reverend Jesse Jackson. When I met with Frank Donatelli of President Reagan's White House Public Liaison staff in July, 1984, he informed me that President Reagan then had an over 50 percent popularity rating among American Jewish voters, the highest such rating ever received by a Republican President. Yet in the November, 1984 election, Reagan received only 35 percent of the Jewish vote. It may be said that in a campaign of abject failure, one of Walter Mondale's few successes was frightening the American Jewish community with the notion that President Reagan posed a threat to their security in the context of the "religion and politics" issue, an issue which I believe was grossly exaggerated and distorted.

Yet while fear for future security has in fact been a strong element of American Jewish voting patterns, this is far from the total explanation. As a conservative political activist who may be termed a specialist in "Jewish politics," I have found that many Jews, including both religious and secular leadership, have come to believe that the post-1960 liberal political agenda is, or should be, an essential part of Jewish religious dogma, tantamount to a modern-day Torah or Talmud. While fear of political conservatism, however, misperceived, may have been the origin of such a theology, there is little doubt that such a theology exists. I have seen this most graphically in supplemental prayers in many synagogues on holidays and Shabbat. These prayers often sound like a reply of the 1960's peace marches and civil rights demonstrations. Perhaps the most extreme example of this is Arthur Waskow's "Freedom Seder," which represents an obscene blending of religion and left-wing radical ideology.

The anti-military and socialist themes inherent in this theology may be traced to the conditions existing for our ancestors under Czarist oppression in Russia, Lithuania, and Poland in the late nineteenth and early twentieth centuries. The Czar's army and the Ukrainian Cossacks were enforcers of pogroms. Therefore, our ancestors understandably developed an anti-military ideology. They thirsted for revolution against their oppressors, and socialism was the prevailing revolutionary ideology of the era.

Yet while it is understandable that our ancestors should have bought their anti-military and socialist ideologies with them to America, it is ludicrous that their descendants should have retained them in our society. The American military has been an instrument of Jewish *liberation*, as exemplified by its destruction of the Nazis in World War II and the airlift of supplies to Israel in order to save the Jewish state during the 1973 Yom Kippur War. Furthermore, it is the American *capitalist* system, and not socialism, which has resulted in the greatest Jewish economic prosperity in the history of Western civilization.

Like many Jewish conservatives, I have dedicated my political life to persuading American Jews of two key assertions. First, while Jews may at one time have had more to fear from American political conservatives than liberals, in our modern political context, American Jewry has far more to fear from the left than from the right. Second, it is high time that American Jews realize that it is not a central tract of the Torah or Talmud that Jews must vote for candidates from the liberal wing of the Democratic party.

Like most Jewish conservatives, my political ideology has been a direct result of my experiences as an

American Jew. In fact, my personal experiences are illustrative of the dilemmas and crucial choices facing the American Jewish voter for the rest of the twentieth century. In essence, my life has been the odyssey of an American Jewish conservative.

I grew up in suburban Pittsburgh, Pennsylvania as the oldest of three children. My father and mother were very involved in the Jewish community as Synagogue president and Hadassah president, respectively. They maintained a Kosher home and taught their children to observe the Shabbat and all Jewish holidays.

My parents' political involvement was limited to voting in elections. They voted the traditional New Deal Democrat line and only deviated to vote for liberal Republicans such as former Pennsylvania U.S. Senator Hugh Scott. Their major political heroes were Franklin and Eleanor Roosevelt, Harry Truman, and above all, Adlai Stevenson. Richard Nixon was tantamount to Haman. Dwight Eisenhower was reviled for his pressure on Israel to withdraw from the Sinai after the 1956 war, although his Democrat Presidential opponent, Adlai Stevenson supported him completely on this.

Like most Jews of their generation, my parents viewed their political beliefs as necessarily intertwined with their future as American Jews. In fact, in 1976, when my mother voted for a Republican presidential candidate, Gerald Ford, for the first and only time in her life, it was due to her belief that the Democratic candidate, Jimmy Carter, a born-again

Christian Evangelist might be inclined to pursue policies detrimental to Jews.

Unlike my parents, I was completely enamored of politics since the age of five, when I actually memorized the names of all our Presidents. I accepted and followed my parents' political beliefs and dreamed of becoming one of our nation's foremost political leaders. Aroused by the charisma of John F. Kennedy and the dreams of the New Frontier and Great Society, I decided at age eleven to pursue a career in law and politics. So it was onward and upward to Northwestern University and the University of Wisconsin Law School to achieve my impossible dream.

At Northwestern and Wisconsin, like most American universities of the late 60's and early 70's, the prevailing academic *zeitgeist* was "radical chic." I would emerge from my years of college and law school, however, as a libertarian conservative. Like many of my fellow "yuppies," I was, in the words of Norman Podhoretz, a liberal who was mugged by reality. Part of this reality was the incredible dichotomy of Jewish campus liberals and radicals who tried to reconcile their left-wing politics with their commitment to the survival of Israel and world Jewry. It has been over ten years since I left the world of the college campus, yet numerous examples of this dichotomy are still vivid in my memory.

I can still remember one of the student leaders of Northwestern's B'nai B'rith Hillel Foundation demonstrating for the removal of the Naval ROTC from campus. Yet this same radical Jewish leader was also active in demanding that the Nixon administration provide Israel with Phantom jets, while he was trying to deprive our own country of one of its most important sources of military officers.

I marched in civil rights marches demonstrating for equal opportunity for black Americans, and I would do so again. Yet I remember at Northwestern a black militant stating in a political science class that black anti-Semitism and anti-Zionism were justified and receiving the support of his black classmates. I then remember a group of black militants wielding baseball bats storming into the Triangle fraternity house, inflicting personal injury and property damage in revenge for an insult allegedly made to a black female by one of the fraternity members. I remember the administration at Northwestern imposing suspensions on these black militants when actually expulsion would have been the proper remedy. Yet I remember seeing Jewish student leaders from the Hillel Foundation demonstrating in support of these same black militants.

I remember the hysteria created by the book, *The Population Bomb* written by Paul Ehrlich, himself a Jew. I remember Jewish professors and student leaders as being in the forefront of the philosophy of families limiting themselves to two children. For world Jewry, however, whose numbers have been decimated in the twentieth century by Hitler's holocaust and the rise of assimilation and intermarriage, such a philosophy is tantamount to suicide.

I remember that universities in the 1930's and 1940's had had a maximum quota for the admission of Jewish students. Yet at the University of Wisconsin Law School, Jewish students were the leaders in the drive to institute a minimum quota for the admission of minority law students. I realized all too well that the quota principle, taken to its *reductio ad absurdum*, would result in a maximum quota for the admission of

Jewish students, a situation which our parents were combatting during their university years.

My experiences as a young Jewish adult were not the only reason I embraced political conservatism. Unlike many of my fellow students, I did not limit myself to reading the works of liberal professors but also avidly studied the writings of such individuals as William F. Buckley, Nobel prize-winning economist Milton Friedman, Norman Podhoretz, Richard Allen, and many others. My experiences as a Jew, however, did persuade me that the political and economic conservatism which I now embraced were particularly beneficial and essential to the welfare of American Jewry as well as the general American society. In essence, by embracing political and economic conservatism, American Jews would both enhance their self-interest as Jews and yet fulfill their altruistic concerns for their non-Jewish fellow Americans. This coincidence of altruism and self-interest is the core of the first chapter of this book.

Chapter 1
Altruism and Self-Interest

"If I am not for myself, who is for me? If I care only for myself, what am I? If not now, when?"
—Hillel, Ethics of the Fathers (Pirke Avot)

Hillel stated this truism 2000 years ago. For the American Jewish conservative, this truism may be translated as follows: What is good for the Jews is also good for America. In the four crucial areas of economics, civil rights, foreign policy, and social issues, the enlightened Jewish self-interest is totally compatible with the American Jew's altruistic concern for his fellow citizens.

American Jews have an interest in a growing economy that will provide sufficient jobs and wealth for the young adult generation to afford more children and still have a surplus to donate to Jewish religious and secular institutions. Such a growing economy results from supply-side economic policies such as Ronald Reagan's tax cuts in the years 1983 and 1984. The Jewish stake in a growing economy is identical to that of the general American community.

American Jews have an interest in a society in which discrimination against, or in favor of, any ethnic group, race or creed will be eliminated. American liberals have attempted to define society by quotas based on ethnic representation. In fact, this dogma was written into the Democratic Party's rules for national convention delegate selection in the years 1972 through 1980. Despite such foolish dogma, however, American Jewish conservatives and their fellow gentile neighbors have overwhelmingly resisted such attempts to guarantee equality of result, as distinguished from equality of opportunity. Both the American Jew and his gentile neighbor remember that a quota can be used to provide a ceiling on ethnic group opportunity as well as a floor.

American Jews have a vital interest in a foreign policy that will guarantee peace through strength. Only by such a policy can America act as a reliable friend of its ally of shared values, the State of Israel. The American gentile community also realizes that peace can only be guaranteed through strength and not through suicidal unilateral disarmament policies. Here again, the Jew's interest in a strong America is identical to that of his gentile neighbors.

Finally, American Jewry has an interest in a society that restores traditional moral values of family, swift justice against criminals, and discipline in our schools. While Jews may differ with such groups as the Moral Majority on certain details, such as the restoration of prayer in public schools, we certainly can find common cause with them in the need to restore traditional societal moral values. Few ethnic groups have been victimized by crime as brutally as urban Jews. The rise in drug usage in our schools has created anguish for middle-class American families, from which Jewish families are hardly immune.

The four previous paragraphs form the core of the ideology of American Jewish conservatives. This is a platform that in no way contradicts the American Jew's concern for fairness towards his fellow citizens of all ethnic groups.

Today, however, a growing number of Jewish liberals are engaging in a vicious assault against the character and motives of American Jewish conservatives. This attack can best be defined as a form of McCarthyism of the Left. It is one thing for American Jewish liberals to attack the validity of the arguments of their Jewish conservative adversaries; it is another thing to engage in an attack upon their character and motives.

Perhaps the best example of this American Jewish liberal onslaught appeared in an article entitled "Behind Jews' Political Principles," written by Rabbi Arthur Hertzberg in *The New York Times* on Friday, November 2, 1984. Rabbi Hertzberg is a highly admirable man who has served as a rabbi of Temple Emanu-El, Englewood, New Jersey and also as president of the American Jewish Congress. He is an individual of high character and his contributions to the welfare of American Jews and the State of Israel are innumerable.

If Jerry Falwell wrote an article criticizing the motives of Christian liberals, I am sure Rabbi Hertzberg would object to it as a merger of religion and politics. Yet Rabbi Hertzberg engaged in this exact same kind of behavior in the aforementioned article where he castigated the motives of Jewish conservatives.

The article was basically an extremely thinly veiled endorsement of Walter Mondale for President. Rabbi Hertzberg wrote: "Today a growing number of middle-class Jews are in revolt against such liberalism. They want to protect their class interest as haves, through alliance with the extreme right. They see little reason to resist creches in public places, prayers in public schools or an anti-abortion amendment. Even the emergence of a right-wing 'Christian America' would be, they argue, a cheap price to pay for support for Israel as a bastion of anti-Communism. Thus, they warn the rest of us not to endanger the Jews' economic and social success by playing too visible a part in battles about the nature of democracy.

"This call for self-interest is still a minority view, but it is troubling indeed. It reduces the meaning of the Jewish struggle in America to a quest for success and abandons those who are still friendless and foreign to fend for themselves...we cannot today join the *forces of selfishness*. We belong with those who cared about us when we were friendless."

Thus, Rabbi Hertzberg has labeled Jews in the conservative movement as virtual apostles of selfishness. Well, Rabbi Hertzberg, we Jewish conservatives *are* concerned about our fellow citizens. And while we respect your motives as a liberal, however much we may disagree about the practical effect of your programs, we certainly wish that you would have an equal respect for our motives as well.

Rabbi Hertzberg, we are concerned about the fact that millions of unskilled black and Hispanic youth are unable to get jobs at the bottom of the corporate ladder, due to the fact that your friends in the labor movement have brought pressure upon Congress to pass minimum wage laws that price the unskilled minority youths out of jobs. Certainly, our minority youth would be better off working for low wages rather than roaming the streets with no jobs at all. Yet the minimum wage laws created by your fellow liberals have basically prevented these youths from attaining the first rung of the ladder, where they might have the opportunity for further advancement.

Rabbi Hertzberg, we are concerned about the fact that your candidate, Walter Mondale, favored policies of tax hikes and protective tariffs, the identical policies followed by Herbert Hoover, resulting in the Great Depression. Certainly, we Jewish conservatives cannot be labeled as selfish for favoring a growing economy instead of high taxes and protective tariffs which would only bring about recession, depression and misery for all our fellow citizens of all ethnic groups.

Rabbi Hertzberg, we Jewish conservatives never thought that it was selfish to support an anti-abortion amendment. We always thought respect for life was at the core of all religious and ethical belief.

Rabbi Hertzberg, you write further in the article that "those who kept the doors closed here argued that new immigrants would do them economic harm. We who lost that fight in the 1930's know that we desecrate our own dead if today we use the economic argument against someone else's claim to life and health." Yes, Rabbi Hertzberg, we Jewish conservatives agree with you that the doors of America should be kept open to new immigrants. Yet, Rabbi Hertzberg, I would remind you that American *conservatives*, such as Patrick Buchanan, the former White House Director of Communications, and Robert L. Bartley, the editor of the *Wall Street Journal*, have been at the forefront of the fight against restrictive immigration bills such as the Simpson-Mazzoli Bill. American conservatives believe that the new immigrants, by and large, have been hard working people who will only nurture the future of America. If you believe that today's conservatives somehow oppose this new immigration, you are barking up the wrong tree.

Rabbi Hertzberg, you then write about the support received by Israel from the conservatives, "No one who remembers the founding of Israel—no one who remembers the moral and political reasons that made that act necessary—can stand by today and watch Israel's meaning traduced by the right. We reject both the fundamentalists who cast it as the major actor in a looming Armageddon and the self-styled political realists who see it leading anti-Soviet interests in the Middle East. After World War II, we did not welcome a new Sparta, we rejoiced in a renewed Jerusalem of justice and peace—and that is still our hope."

Well, Rabbi Hertzberg, your hope of a renewed Jerusalem of justice and peace is altogether admirable. I am reminded, however, of the quote from the prophet Jeremiah, "Saying peace, peace, when there is no peace." As long as there is a Soviet Union feeding weapons to the Syrians and the PLO, we will never see a Jerusalem of peace and justice. My "self-styled political realist" friends on the right support Israel, while the liberal members of the National Council of Churches have acted against the interests of Israel wherever possible. So, Rabbi Hertzberg, you shall search in vain for support for Israel among Christian liberal clergy, while I shall say to my friends in the Christian right who support Israel, "Praise the Lord, and pass the ammunition."

Rabbi Hertzberg, the reason that a growing number of Jews have left the theology of liberalism is that we have a different historical memory than you. We know that to combat and deter the evils of Soviet communist totalitarianism, the United States must have a strong military, just as it was necessary to have a strong military to defeat the evil totalitarianism of the Nazis. Above all, Rabbi Hertzberg, we know that

American Jews succeeded in this nation not because of what government did for people but because of what people did for themselves. We see government as constituting an *obstacle* to the upward mobility of our friends among other minority groups. We know that we Jews rose up from the sweatshop, as described in the next chapter, because we lived in a society where there was no welfare state to discourage initiative, where there was no excessive regulation to burden small businesses, and where there were no runaway taxes and inflation to destroy the Jewish entrepreneur before he climbed the ladder of success. No, Rabbi Hertzberg, we Jewish conservatives are not selfish in spite of your deplorable attack upon our motives; indeed, we see our self-interest as Jews as totally compatible with our concern for our fellow Americans.

Chapter 2
Up From the Sweatshop

Most of the people in these neighborhoods were manual workers—skilled, but manual—and even though statistically categorized as "white collar" were often push cart peddlers, butchers, grocers, or in other occupations where book learning was of no economic value... While some teachers spoke glowingly of the Lower East Side Jewish children, others found teaching them to be "unusually tedious" and observed that "many come from families in which English is seldom spoken at all, and where good manners and cleanliness are decidedly at a discount..." This was an era when it was common to avoid promoting children until their scholastic performance merited it, but even so the record of Polish Jews was worse than others. A 1911 study showed that 41 percent of the 5,431 Russian Jewish children surveyed were behind the "normal grade level."
—Thomas Sowell, in *Ethnic America*

Almost every American Jewish family of Eastern European origin has the historical memory of the "sweatshop." Jewish grandfathers have told their grandchildren their story of arriving at Ellis Island in anticipation that they would soon find the streets of Manhattan to be covered with gold. Instead, these immigrants, who as a rule only spoke Yiddish and possessed a minimal education, would soon face the reality of the sweatshop.

In the sweatshop, the Jewish immigrant found oppressive working conditions and little pay. In the new "golden medina," however, the Jew had hope which he never possessed in Eastern Europe. At long last he was free. He had in most cases arrived in

America with little or no working skills; accordingly, he was forced to find work in the sweatshop. He at least, however, could find work, since there was no minimum wage law that priced this unskilled immigrant out of the job market. In the sweatshop, he was in many cases able to work his way up the ladder of business to a skilled position. There was no bilingual education system in the public schools, so he was forced to learn English rapidly, which would benefit him greatly in his economic and personal life. The levels of taxation and inflation were relatively low, so he could start a business of his own, free from excessive government regulation. Finally there was no welfare state, so the Jewish immigrant had to work in order to support his family. Since there was no welfare system that rewarded families in which the father had left the home, the Jewish immigrant had one incentive: to stay with his family, to work hard, and to build a good future for his children in the New Land.

I am often genuinely puzzled that today's Jewish liberal has completely forgotten that it was precisely this absence of the liberal agenda that enabled American Jewish immigrants to "make it" in society in the late 19th and early 20th centuries. From my own experience, I can only say "baruch ha-shem"—praise the Lord—that my two grandfathers arrived in this country before the advent of the welfare state.

I say this since in my own lifetime, I have seen the welfare state totally destroy the dreams and aspirations of the so-called new emerging minorities, the blacks and Hispanics. Jewish liberals in a subtle, subconsciously racist way think that we Jews have "made it," and the blacks "haven't" because we Jews have a heritage of a more stable family environment. Thus, the argument continues, we must compensate the black for this disadvantage by providing him with the dubious benefit of the welfare system that provides for the black urban poor from the cradle to the grave.

This line of reasoning is not only insulting to the American black; it also totally ignores historical reality. As the distinguished black economist Walter Williams has noted, up until the 1930's the American black family was remarkably stable in spite of the pre-Civil War heritage of slavery, which often resulted in the decimation of the black family. The illegitimacy rate among black children was in fact far lower than that of the white community until the 1940's.

The development of the welfare state changed all this. Prior to its advent, American blacks were impoverished and brutalized due to a malignant and virulent societal and institutional racism. Against this scourge, the black American could not find protection in the statutes or the courts. Nevertheless, he persevered in the hope that both the laws and attitudes of society someday would change.

To a certain extent, that day finally did arrive in the second half of the twentieth century. The Supreme Court held in *Brown vs. Board of Education* that de jure racial segregation was unconstitutional. The 1964 Civil Rights Act outlawed employment discrimination on the basis of race. Finally, although societal racism was far from eliminated, employers and institutions opened the doors to admittance of blacks at an unprecedented and rapid rate. Now, however, the blacks were faced with a new scourge that had never menaced the American Jew, the scourge of the all encompassing welfare state.

Few writers have illustrated this better than Charles A. Murray, author of the highly acclaimed book, *Losing Ground*. As Dr. Murray pointed out in a

1982 Heritage Foundation publication entitled *Safety Nets and the Truly Needy* , prior to 1960, the function of social welfare in our society was to provide a modest amount of money, just enough for the bare necessities, to those who otherwise would be destitute, to wit, a dole. Such recipients included those who could not care for themselves, such as the aged, the disabled, the temporarily unemployed, and the perennially destitute. Thus, as Dr. Murray states, the four principal programs comprising the safety net were Social Security, Aid to Families with Dependent Children (A.F.D.C.), unemployment insurance, and workers' compensation.

The Kennedy-Johnson years inaugurated an entire change of philosophy regarding welfare. Whereas welfare had previously been regarded by Americans of all races as a stigma to be avoided, the New Frontier-Great Society philosophy was that welfare should no longer be regarded as a stigma but as an entitlement of all American citizens. Various restrictions and investigations were to be eliminated. Rather than a program to provide for the bare necessities for those who could not care for themselves due to no fault of their own, welfare was now regarded as a right by everyone to receive from the public treasury a decent standard of living.

Thus, in terms of 1980 dollars, Federal welfare programs rose from 7.9 billion dollars in 1950 to 244.4 billion dollars in 1980. Whereas the four programs mentioned before had constituted 91 percent of the "safety net" budget in 1950, these four programs only constituted 63 percent of the 1980 "safety net" budget.

With the growth of welfare allotments and the elimination of its stigmas, impoverished Americans, both black and white, found a new incentive to avoid work and maximize one's welfare eligibility. Such maximization of benefits often resulted when a father left the mother of his children, whether or not he was married to her. Thus, the welfare system accomplished very quickly what slavery had been unable to do for over 200 years, namely, the decimation and destruction of the black family.

Prior to the advent of our modern welfare system, black families were noteworthy in their stress of the work ethic. Now, among many urban blacks, this pride and work ethic were replaced by a "welfare culture." In such an environment, as Dr. Murray has shown, there was a decline in "job readiness," which is defined by him as socialization of the individual in the basics of a job culture. Job readiness is almost always present in families in which the children grow up with parents who are employed. In the new urban ghetto welfare culture, however, job readiness decreased to such an extent that an underclass of Americans developed that did not possess the basic rudiments of obtaining and holding a job; such as getting up for work every day, accepting the instructions of leaders, and believing in the notion of a reward for a hard day's work. This decline in job readiness has been most vividly illustrated by author Ken Auletta in his book, *The Underclass.*

In such an environment, the various government subsidized job training programs were bound to fail, since many of those targeted by these programs lacked job readiness. Furthermore, those urban black residents who really wanted to work and hold jobs often found themselves hit with a double whammy. Societal racism had resulted in blacks receiving an inferior education. The minimum wage law had resulted in the undereducated and consequently unskilled urban minorities being priced out of jobs by high minimum wages. This eliminated the best form of job training: on-the-job training whereby unskilled laborers could learn skills and advance up the system.

It is no wonder that Nobel prize-winning economist Milton Friedman has stated that if the minimum wage law had been in effect when our grandparents came to this country, they would have been unable to obtain a job. One may infer that if the welfare system and minimum wage laws had been in effect when Jews began arriving to America in massive numbers in the late 19th and early 20th century, we may well have witnessed terrible damage to the Jewish family and a massive retardation in Jewish economic progress. In short, the Jew would have taken much longer to emerge from the sweatshop if he had even had the opportunity to get a job there.

Even more disheartening to American blacks who wish to form their own businesses is the existence of burdensome government regulations and high taxes that make it impossible to form a new enterprise. I often wonder if my grandfathers would have been able to start their businesses in today's economic environment of burdensome regulation and high taxes. To right this historical wrong, American conservatives have proposed the best remedy, to wit, the creation of enterprise zones where minority members may create businesses and receive substantial tax and regulatory exemptions.

Yet what is the American Jewish liberal's response? He has totally forgotten his own heritage, and proposes to "help" America's emerging minorities by the creation of more welfare programs and higher taxes. Rarely has this been more graphically exhibited than in an article in the *New York Times* on January 20, 1986 written by Albert Vorspan, a prominent Jewish liberal employed by the Union of American Hebrew Congregations. In an article entitled "What He Meant to Jews" commemorating the birthday of Dr. Martin Luther King, Jr., Vorspan contended that Jews and blacks shared a common agenda of resisting the Reagan program of budgetary cuts in the welfare programs. Somehow, I fail to see in the Torah or Talmud any doctrine that mandated opposition to the Reagan budget program. These holy Jewish books speak of helping the poor, but they do not speak of helping the poor person to such an extend that he has no incentive to work. With friends like Mr. Vorspan, thoughtful American blacks hardly need any enemies.

A word must also be said with regard to the plight of American Hispanics. Hispanics in large part face the same difficulties as blacks with one significant addition. Hispanic immigrants have a dire need to learn English in order to succeed in our society. Instead, they are granted the dubious gift of a bilingual education system which fools Hispanic youth into thinking that they can function in our society by simply using Spanish, without any necessity of really learning English.

As the prominent New York educator Howard Hurwitz has pointed out, nothing is more counterproductive to the welfare of Hispanic youth. These youth should go to a school where only English is used so that they will absolutely be smothered with English and forced to learn it. This is not to say that in their own homes they should forsake Spanish language and culture. One of the joys of my youth was listening to my grandparents speak Yiddish in conjunction with their observance of the Jewish way of life. However, I'm quite grateful that my grandparents did not attend a bilingual education school but instead were forced to learn English in the public schools, where the teachers did not speak Yiddish.

I do not accuse the American Jewish liberal of approaching urban minorities with bad intentions. I do accuse him of forgetting the American heritage that resulted in his success. Our urban minorities do not need more welfarism; they need more capitalism.

And to paraphrase Tevye in *Fiddler on the Roof*, if capitalism is a curse, our urban minorities should be smitten with it. American Jews have already been subject to the curse of capitalism, and as a result, we have prospered in American society to an extent unparalleled anywhere else in our history.

Chapter 3
The Economics of American-Jewish Survival

"Where there is no budget, there is no Torah."
—Anonymous

"Let somebody else seek zero population growth. We Jews lost one-third of our population in the Holocaust, and we need more people."
—Rabbi Albert Lewis, Temple Beth Sholom, Haddon Heights, New Jersey

"Burn Jews, not oil."
—Anti-Semitic slogan found on bumper sticker during 1973 Arab oil embargo.

The above three quotations in a nutshell display the three crucial economic issues affecting the future of the American Jewish community. In order to maintain synagogues and institutions of Jewish learning, young Jewish families must obtain sufficient wealth to both maintain a family and make contributions to Jewish religious, educational, and charitable institutions. In a century of the holocaust, assimilations and intermarriage, Jews need to have larger and not smaller families in order to maintain their numbers and political power. Finally, Jews must promote economic policies that result in energy independence for our nation in order that we may remain free of the blackmail of the Arab oil cartel. Yet in almost every case, liberal American Jewish politicians have promoted policies directly contrary to these three needs.

It is no accident that in both his Presidential campaigns, Ronald Reagan received his strongest support from individuals under the age of 35. The inflation of the 1970's had resulted in young professionals just out of college being escalated into tax brackets that their parents at a corresponding age had never faced. While our welfare system was encouraging the least educated segment of our youth to have children out of wedlock, high inflation and high tax rates were forcing the best and brightest of our young people to defer the decision to have children. The impact of this was most severely felt among young Jewish couples. In fact, the Jewish birthrate was reduced to an all-time low of 1.5 children per family.

Thus, for the young Jewish family, the Reagan economic program was a godsend. The implementation of reduced marginal tax rates and indexation for inflation gave the young, upwardly mobile Jewish family the ability to have children and obtain a sufficient surplus to contribute economically to the welfare of the entire Jewish community. Yet few groups were more outspoken in their opposition to the Reagan economic program than Jewish liberal politicians and liberal Jewish organizations.

The most vigorous contention of these Jewish opponents to Reaganomics was that the cut of the top tax bracket from 70 to 50 percent would reduce for the wealthy the benefit of charitable giving, since the tax refund per dollar of charitable donations would be reduced from 70 cents to 50 cents. This argument overlooked the fact that the wealthiest members of both Jewish and non-Jewish society tend to favor such charities as orchestras and art museums over religious institutions, whose major contributors are the middle class. Aside from this, however, the liberal Jewish argument proved to be way wide of the mark in practice.

As pointed out by James Keller in the Heritage Foundation magazine *Policy Review* in the winter of 1986, charitable donations rose from 49 billion dollars in 1980 to an all-time high of 75 billion dollars in 1984. Furthermore, the 1984 level of charitable contributions was the highest such level as a percentage of personal income in fifteen years. The reasons for this were not hard to discern. Charitable contributions have always risen with the growth of disposable personal income, which happened during the years of the Reagan economic recovery. As Pat McClenic, the United Way's Acting Director for Public Relations states, "When you have more, you tend to give more."

It is indeed illogical that Jewish liberals could expect that a Jewish middle-class afflicted with high tax rates could also make high contributions to Jewish charities. The reduction in these tax rates could only serve to benefit the level of such donations.

There is, however, an even more pressing form of tax relief needed for young Jewish families, to wit, tuition tax credits for Jewish and non-Jewish families who send their children to private elementary and secondary schools. In an American society where pressures for assimilation are enormous, the Jewish day-school is a vital institution in educating the next generation in the joys and beauty of the Jewish way of life. Yet few individuals have been more vocal in their opposition to tuition tax credits than Jewish liberals.

Such Jewish liberal politicians base their opposition on an assertion that tuition tax credits for people who send their children to private religious schools represent a form of direct state aid to religious institutions, thus violating the First Amendment mandate of separation of church and state. This argument, however, on its face is absolutely ludicrous. If there was any validity to it, then the G.I. Bill of Rights, which provides for the payment of tuition for veterans to attend all universities, religious or secular, would have to be declared unconstitutional. Courts and legislators alike have always recognized the crucial and significant distinction between aid to the student and direct aid to the educational institution. Otherwise, a veteran who wished to attend either Yeshiva University or Notre Dame could not receive G.I. Bill assistance.

On every Shabbat when Rabbi Albert L. Lewis of Temple Beth Sholom, Haddon Heights, New Jersey officiates at a naming of a baby girl, he congratulates the couple and implores them to have more children so that the infant may have many brothers and sisters. Then, Rabbi Lewis pleads with the congregation to encourage the growth of the Jewish birth rate. No thinking Jew can dispute the good Rabbi. Hitler's Holocaust resulted in the elimination of one-third of the world's Jewish population. Intermarriage and assimilation are twin cancers eating away at the numerical growth and development of the American Jewish community.

Yet in his quest, Rabbi Lewis faces overwhelming obstacles. Not only are young Jewish families economically deterred from having children by liberal economic policies of high taxation and inflation; they are also *intellectually* persuaded not to have more children by the liberal ideology of "zero population growth." The father of this movement was none other than a Jewish liberal, Paul Ehrlich, author of *The Population Bomb.*

It is beyond the scope of this work to dwell at length on the dubious arguments advanced by Dr. Ehrlich that the world birth rate is threatening to bring about the destruction of our planet. Various political commentators and demographers, such as Ben Wattenberg, have ably demonstrated the flaws in Dr. Ehrlich's argument. One thing, however, is abundantly clear. Those Jews who adopt the Ehrlich ideology as part and parcel of Jewish theology are sowing the seeds of the destruction of the numerical existence of the American Jewish community.

There is a third economic issue which affects not only the internal welfare of the American Jewish community but also the ability of the United States to aid the State of Israel, namely, the energy issue. There is no tenet of American liberal philosophy that has been more counterproductive to the welfare of our society and the State of Israel than the implementation of price controls on oil. Since the days of the Emperor Diocletian in ancient Rome, price controls have always resulted in an increase in demand and a decrease in productivity, thus resulting in severe shortages. This was exactly the case in the 1970's when oil price controls resulted in a decrease in domestic petroleum extraction, resulting in increasing dependence on Arab oil.

Throughout this period, conservatives like Milton Friedman argued for total decontrol. They asserted that while there would be an immediate sharp increase in oil prices, this would be temporary, as numerous domestic producers would now increase production. This would result in a permanent decrease in the price of domestic oil, further bringing down foreign oil prices. When Ronald Reagan removed all price controls on domestically extracted oil in 1981, this is exactly what happened. Today, the United States is far less dependent on Arab oil than ever, and the price of oil is falling below $10.00 per barrel as the Saudis endeavor to undercut both American and foreign oil producers.

Thus, the free market has been the greatest guarantor of American energy independence, enabling the Reagan administration to pursue an unequivocal pro-Israel foreign policy. Yet in spite of this, Jewish liberals such as Senator Howard Metzenbaum (D-Ohio) actually advocated continuing controls on the price of oil at the time of President Reagan's decontrol in 1981. Such continuing control would have been a total disaster for the State of Israel, as United States domestic oil production would have continued to be abysmal, thus resulting in a continued reliance on Arab oil.

Perhaps Senator Metzenbaum and other Jewish liberals mean well. But their well-meaning cures in economic matters are often worse than the disease.

Chapter 4
Israel, Neo-Isolationism,
and Neo-Pacifism

"We say to our brother, Arafat, that Nicaragua is his land and the PLO cause is the cause of the Sandinistas."
—Thomas Borge, Interior Minister of Nicaragua on welcoming Yasser Arafat to Managua on the first anniversary of the Sandinista Revolution in 1980.

"The links between us are not new, your comrades did not come to our country just to train, but also to fight."
—Yasser Arafat, in responding to Thomas Borge's above quote.

"Dear Commandante—We want to commend you and the members of your government for taking steps to open up the political process in your country. The Nicaraguan people have not had the opportunity to participate in a genuinely free election for over fifty years. We support your decision to schedule elections this year, to reduce press censorship, and to allow greater freedom of assembly for political parties. Finally, we recognize that you have taken steps in the midst of ongoing military hostilities on the borders of Nicaragua."
—Quote from letter to Daniel Ortega, dictator of Nicaragua, signed by ten members of the United States House of Representatives, including Representative Stephen J. Solarz (D-New York).

Stephen Solarz often portrays himself as Israel's champion in the United States House of Representatives. Yet his votes against aid to the Contras and his propitiation of the Sandinista regime, as quoted above, have helped to insure the survival of one of the most anti-Semitic governments in the world and the PLO's number one ally in the Western Hemisphere.

Tragically, however, Stephen Solarz is not alone among Jews in the United States House of Representatives. He is one of five liberal Democratic Jewish members of the House of Representatives whom can be best labeled, for want of a better term, as the Jewish Liberal Congressional Establishment. The other members of this elite group include Representatives Mel Levine and Henry Waxman of California, Samuel Gejdenson of Connecticut, and Theodore Weiss of New York. All five of these individuals style themselves as great defenders of the existence and survival of the State of Israel and actively court Jewish organizational support.

The sad fact of the matter is, however, that all five of these representatives subscribe to the ideology described by former United Nations Ambassador Jeane Kirkpatrick as Blame American First. This is a post-Viet Nam ideology that finds fault with almost every effort to improve our military defense posture. This ideology further terms as "aggression" efforts to aid revolutionary freedom fighters against Communist totalitarianism, such as the Contras. This is an ideology that even went so far as to attempt to undermine American efforts to assist democrats (with a small "d") such as Jose Napoleon Duarte in El Salvador to combat the terrors of both the Reactionary right and the Communist left.

This liberal "gang of five" is in reality the direct political descendant of the isolationists and neo-pacifists of the 1930's, who were led by Representative Hamilton Fish (R-New York) and Senator Gerald Nye (R-Montana). Just as Solarz and his fellow members of the Jewish Liberal Congressional Establishment favor accommodation with the Sandinistas, Fish and Nye favored a hands-off attitude regarding Nazi aggression in Europe. Just as these five Representatives vilify the "military-industrial complex," Nye and Fish vilified the so-called "merchants of death" of the 1930's.

The deleterious effect of the ideology of Blame America First on American foreign policy is obvious. What is less obvious to both American Jewry and the American electorate at large is the absolutely ruinous effect this ideology has on the future survival and security of the State of Israel.

The first such effect is political. The American gentile can justifiably ask the members of the Jewish Liberal Congressional Establishment the following question: Your policies, in essence, call for American unilateral disarmament and an isolationist policy of military withdrawal from various areas of the world. Why then do you make an exception of Israel by advocating increasing American aid to the Jewish State? In positioning themselves as spokesmen for the American Jewish community at large, these five Congressmen mislead the American gentile public into believing that all American Jews share this hypocrisy, in spite of the fact that the overwhelming silent majority of American Jews are patriotic citizens who support American efforts to defend ourselves and freedom for other peoples against Soviet encroachment throughout the world.

This political problem for American Jewry, however, is minor compared to the direct harm inflicted, albeit unintentionally, by these Congressional Jewish liberals on Israeli security interests. This damage comes at a time when there has never been a greater convergence and confluence of American and Israeli foreign policy interests, particularly in three areas:

1. The greatest threat to American national security is the growth of Soviet conventional and nuclear forces, particularly as the Soviets approach a first-strike capability to destroy the American nuclear deterrent before it can respond to a Soviet attack. Likewise, the Soviet Union and its client states in the Middle East, particularly Syria and Iraq, represent the greatest danger to the long-term survival of Israel.

2. Israel faces a continuing war against the terrorism of the PLO, which receives aid and assistance from a whole network of terrorist states throughout the world, of which Nicaragua is a leading member. Likewise, American national security is directly threatened by the terrorist Nicaraguan Sandinista state which is attempting to spread a "revolution without borders" throughout Central America and Mexico.

3. The Strategic Defense Initiative, labeled pejoratively as "star wars" by the liberals, while not a foolproof protection of American population centers, definitely offers America the realistic expectation of shielding our nuclear arsenal against any attempted Soviet first strike attack. Likewise, the Strategic Defense Initiative offers Israel its best hope of defense against Soviet SS-21's that Russia has supplied to Syria. This is why Israel has volunteered itself as a subcontractor in the Strategic Defense Initiative program.

Yet how do members of the Jewish Liberal Congressional Establishment vote? They consistently vote against efforts to increase our defense capability against the Soviet Union, the arch enemy of both America and Israel. They consistently vote against efforts to aid the freedom fighters in Nicaragua against Sandinista terrorism. Finally, they oppose expansion of the Strategic Defense Initiative program, in spite of the salvation it may offer Israel against Syrian missiles speeding toward Israeli population centers. And as one examines each of these three issues in depth, one's bewilderment with these five representatives evolves into contempt.

An April 26, 1986 *New York Times* article described a Talmud class that is attended by a number of Jewish members of Congress. At one such class, the Rabbi conducted a discussion of Amalek, a Biblical tribe that was constantly committing atrocities against Jews. Representative Gejdenson joked, "Can Ronald Reagan's 'evil empire' be Amalek?"

Obviously, Mr. Gejdenson meant to poke fun at President Reagan's reference to the Soviet Union as an "evil empire." But Mr. Gejdenson, your joke is not very funny. If anything, President Reagan's reference to the Soviet Union as an "evil empire" was too kind.

Mr. Gejdenson, you must have forgotten that within the past decade, the Soviet Union has committed genocide against the Afghan people; including the use of such tactics as booby trapping toys of children. Mr. Gejdenson, you forget that this is the same Soviet Union that plotted through its Bulgarian surrogates the attempted assassination of Pope John Paul II. You also forget that this is the same Soviet Union that has used yellow rain toxins to kill dissident Hmong tribesmen in Laos. Why don't you, Mr. Gejdenson, ask people who long for freedom in Poland, Czechoslovakia and Hungary whether they think Mr. Reagan's designation of the Soviet Union as an "evil empire" is inaccurate?

For Jewry, the aggressive and totalitarian nature of the Soviet Union is even more apparent. This is a nation where anti-Semitism and anti-Zionism are official policy. For those Jews who wish to leave this Gulag, the road to emigration is a nightmare.

For those Jews who are lucky enough to emigrate from the Soviet Union and find repatriation in Israel, the Soviet Union still remains an ominous presence. It is the Soviet Union that basically provides the training and armament for the PLO and its associated world terror network. For Syria and Iraq, it is the Soviet Union that is the arsenal of totalitarianism and Israel's destruction.

The Jewish liberal will accuse me of using inflammatory language and possessing a "cold war mentality." One must remember, however, that for the Soviet Union, the cold war has never ended. It is only in the self-delusion of liberal western minds that the Soviet Union has somehow become less aggressive.

Jewish liberals have been prominent in the various disarmament campaigns during the past decade. They somehow fail to realize that it is the presence of our defense establishment that has deterred the Soviet Union from further aggression and warfare. It is not the presence of arms that creates wars, but rather a strategic imbalance between two nations with political differences. The Jewish liberals, above all, should be aware of this and cease their fuzzy and utopian vision of placing our children's future in paper arms control treaties with the Soviet Union. Indeed, as evidenced by the construction of phased-array radar in Siberia, in violation of the SALT Treaty, cheating is the hallmark of Soviet "arms control" policies. And if the Jewish liberal needs be reminded of the ultimate character of Soviet aggression, anti-Zionism and anti-Semitism, he now only needs to look southward on our doorstep at Nicaragua.

When one examines the domestic and foreign policies of the Sandinista regime, aid to the Contras becomes an American moral imperative. When one examines the anti-Semitic and anti-Israeli policies of the Sandinista regime, aid to the Contras indeed becomes a *Jewish* moral imperative.

The Sandinistas obtained the support of the Nicaraguan populace in their 1978-1979 revolution due to the harsh authoritarian and corrupt nature of the Somoza regime. Unfortunately, the Sandinista regime is even worse. The massive waves of Miskito refugees fleeing Sandinista attacks, the censorship of La Prensa, and the closing of the Catholic Church radio station all bear witness to the fact that the Sandinista revolution is one that betrayed the very people it ostensibly pledged to liberate.

In July, 1985, Alvaro Baldizon Aviles, who had been serving as chief investigator for the Nicaraguan Interior Ministry's Special Investigation Committee, defected to the United States. He substantiated the continuing Sandinista reign of terror, including the assassination of political opponents and the beating and torture of dissidents. He also added evidence to the charge that the Sandinista regime is heavily involved in drug trafficking. Mr. Baldizon, who worked directly under Thomas Borge, the Interior Minister, stated that Mr. Borge himself had transported bags of cocaine as part of a smuggling operation.

Unfortunately, this regime is not content to confine its barbarism within its borders. Instead, Mr. Ortega and Mr. Borge have put into practice their theology of a "revolution without borders" by assisting Communist revolutionaries in El Salvador. Furthermore, the Sandinista regime, as described at the beginning of this chapter, is an active ally of the PLO world terror network.

It is little wonder that a revolution against such a sadistic regime should arise. In spite of the outrageous liberal falsehood that the Contras are merely a small band of Somocistas sponsored by the United States, the Contras actually have a force of over twenty thousand freedom fighters, a larger number than the Sandinistas had when Somoza fled in 1979. As Assistant Secretary of State for Inter-American Affairs, Elliott Abrams wrote in the *Miami Herald* on Sunday, May 4, 1986, the fact that the Contras have not yet won is a reflection of the Soviet and Cuban arming and training of a Sandinista army at least six times larger than anything Somoza ever had.

The American liberal response to the call for Contra aid had been a campaign of slander and libel unmatched in recent American history. The big liberal lie is the statement that the Contras are composed of and led by former Somocista guardsmen. The overwhelming number of Contras, however, are under nineteen years of age. This means that they were actually only twelve years old when Somoza left power! One would suppose that the liberals will next tell us that Somoza had a repressive army of twelve-year-old national guardsmen. As for the leadership of the Contras, it has been almost entirely composed of men who participated in the revolution against Somoza and have been appalled by Sandinista repression.

Thus, the Contras deserve the support of all ethnic groups purely on humanitarian grounds alone. When one examines Sandinista policy towards Jewry and the State of Israel, Jewish support for the Contras becomes an absolute moral imperative.

Sandinista Nicaragua, like modern Poland, is a land of anti-Semitism without Jews. The Jewish community in Nicaragua was never larger than fifty families at its peak. Yet as documented by the Anti-Defamation League (ADL) of B'nai B'rith in a "White Paper on the Sandinistas and Jews" published on March 19, 1986, virtually this entire community fled Nicaragua after the fall of Somoza as a result of Sandinista anti-Semitic threats and harassment. This campaign of Nazi-style terrorism was highlighted by the Sandinista fire bombing of the synagogue in Managua in 1978 while the congregation was worshipping inside. As described by the ADL White Paper, congregants attempting to flee were confronted by armed Sandinistas who ordered them not to leave the burning building.

Certainly, nobody will accuse the ADL of being a right-wing organization. The ADL report further described the alliance of terror between the Sandinistas and the PLO. The Sandinistas authorized the opening of a PLO embassy in Managua, while at the same time they broke diplomatic relations with Israel and supported efforts to expel Israel from the United Nations.

The ADL report further documented joint Sandinista-PLO military activities in Jordan in the early 1970's during the "Black September" battles. In

1980 PLO members went to Nicaragua to supervise military training.

A 1983 *Wall Street Journal* article entitled "The Sandinistas and the Jews" by Shoshana Bryen further documented Sandinista-PLO military collaboration. Libya, Algeria and the PLO played principal roles in arming the Sandinistas in their revolt against Somoza, and after the revolution, the PLO lent the Sandinista government nearly $12,000,000. In January, 1982 the PLO sent pilots to Nicaragua and guerrilla fighters to El Salvador.

Yet Sandinista anti-Semitism cannot simply be rationalized as anti-Zionism. Nicaraguan Foreign Minister Miguel D'Escoto was quoted in the *Washington Post* on January 27, 1985 as stating, "I remembered that it was the Levites in the synagogue who crucified our Lord." *Nuevo Diario*, a Managua newspaper which, according to the ADL report, closely adheres to the Sandinista line, stated on July 17, 1982 that "the world's money, banking and finance are in the hands of descendants of Jews, the eternal protectors of Zionism. Consequently, controlling economic power, they control political power as now happens in the United States."

In the face of this overwhelmingly clear and convincing record of Sandinista anti-Semitism, and the compelling case for support of the Contra freedom fighters, how did the five aforesaid members of the Jewish Liberal Congressional Establishment, to wit, Representatives Gejdenson, Solarz, Waxman, Levine, and Weiss vote in 1985 on the question of Contra aid?

All five of these individuals noted "no." In a case of absolute moral disgrace, Representative Weiss in 1984 voted against a foreign aid bill which included 2.1

billion dollars worth of aid to Israel on the basis that the bill included aid for the Contras as well.

These five individuals are free to vote their consciences as they see fit. By their vote, however, in denying aid to rebels fighting one of the most anti-Semitic and anti-Israel regimes in the world, they prove that their loyalty to liberalism superseded any loyalty they had toward Jewry and the State of Israel. In short, they lost all moral authority to act as spokesmen for Jewry, and they proved once and for all that modern liberalism is totally antithetical to the best interests of American Jewry and the State of Israel.

There remains, however, a footnote on this issue in which a liberal rabbi committed the ultimate disgrace against his own people. I speak of Rabbi Balfour Brickner of the Stephen Wise Free Synagogue in New York, who stated that in two visits to Nicaragua he had found no evidence of persecution of Jews.

Rabbi Brickner's actions are even more frightening than those of the Jewish Liberal Congressional Establishment. The acts of politicians, however foolish, do not have the moral force of religion behind them. When a clergyman like Rabbi Brickner can be deceived by the Sandinistas and then use the moral authority of his pulpit to persuade Jews to oppose aid to freedom fighters against the leading apostles of anti-Semitism in the Western Hemisphere, you have the ultimate act of political masochism.

Yet the neo-pacifists continue their campaign to capture American foreign policy, with the full cooperation and support of the Liberal Jewish community. They oppose the Strategic Defense Initiative, labeling it as "star wars." By doing so, they threaten the future security of the State of Israel as well as that of that of the United States.

On May 16, 1986, Israeli Defense Minister Yitzhak Rabin and United States Defense Secretary Caspar Weinberger executed at the Pentagon a memorandum of understanding on Israel's participation in research on the Strategic Defense Initiative. This participation came as no surprise to those who have followed the history of SDI. An article in the *New York Times* on Sunday, March 9, 1986, by Henry Kamm quoted Lt. General James J. Abrahamson, Director of SDI, as stating that Prime Minister Peres, several ministers, the Chief of Staff, and Israeli private industry were very supportive of Israeli participation in the program.

According to this *Times* article, Israeli strategic analysts place a high priority on anti-missile defense of urban centers. It further stated that Israel saw the program as having highly beneficial spin-off effects on civilian industry. As a close aid to Shimon Peres states, "If Reagan had not come up with SDI for any other reason, he should have done it for Shimon Peres alone."

Jewish and gentile liberals in the Congress have placed a high priority in defeating this very program which promises such a great benefit to the people of Israel. Hopefully, they will continue to be unsuccessful. Otherwise, if some day Soviet SS-21's launched by Syria reach Israeli population centers undefended by strategic defense weapons, American liberals will have the blood of Israelis on their hands.

Chapter 5
The Evangelist Right: The Liberal Jew's Bogeyman

"Dr. Jerry, please explain to the American people the truth about
our involvement in Lebanon"
—telephone conversation between Israeli Prime Minister
Menachem Begin and Dr. Jerry Falwell, 1982.

As every Jew who is over the age of five knows,
there has been no more fervent opponent of anti-
Semitism in all forms than former Israeli Prime Minister Menachem Begin. During his tenure as Israeli
Prime Minister, Begin formed a very close relationship
with Dr. Jerry Falwell, the Evangelist Reverend
whose leadership of the Moral Majority and his syndi-
cated television show have, in the eyes of most American political observers, made him the leader of the
Christian Evangelist Right political activist movement. It is almost inconceivable that Menachem Begin
would form a close personal and political relationship
with Falwell if the Reverend was an anti-Semite and
a threat to the well-being of American Jews.

But if you believe television producer Norman Lear
and his organization, People for the American Way,
the American Jewish Congress, or Rabbis Balfour
Brickner and David Saperstein, Jerry Falwell is a
mortal danger to American Jews. Such individuals
and groups all scared the living hell out of the majority
of American Jews in 1984 to vote for Walter Mondale
on the basis that Ronald Reagan and his friend, Jerry

Falwell, were illegitimately combining religion with politics. Never mind the fact that liberal clergymen have been involved for years in politics, including such anti-Zionist clergymen as the Berrigan brothers and William Sloane Coffin, without such people as Rabbis Brickner and Saperstein uttering a word of criticism. Never mind the fact that liberal Christian organizations such as the National Council of Churches have gone on record with pro-PLO pronouncements, without Norman Lear saying a word about this combination of religion and politics! What really disturbs Messrs. Lear, Brickner and Saperstein is that Jerry Falwell is a Reverend who does not carry a membership in the Democratic Party, but instead interprets his religious liturgy as compelling him to dissent from the liberal clergy party line.

It is beyond the scope of this chapter to analyze every position that Jerry Falwell has taken regarding Jews and Judaism. I would heartily recommend, however, that any fair-minded Jew read the book, *Jerry Falwell and the Jews* by Merrill Simon, the National Political Editor of *Israel Today*. In this book, Reverend Falwell answered a wide variety of questions regarding Jews and Judaism. Far from being a defamer of Judaism, Falwell perhaps more than any other Christian clergyman stresses the Judaic origins of Christianity; in fact, almost all of his sermons on values stress the *"Judeo-Christian"* heritage. Far from being an anti-Semite, Reverend Falwell has been an active combatant of anti-Semitism in all forms and places; for example, his organizational newspapers have devoted much time and space to exposing the anti-Semitism present in Assad's Syria, as opposed to various documentaries of networks such as CBS which have attempted to promote the idea that the Syrians are only anti-Zionist and not anti-Semitic. Finally, both in the Simon book and his various sermons down through the years, Falwell has been second to none in his support for the State of Israel.

Despite this record, however, Falwell's enemies in the Jewish community have kept up their Mc-Carthyite attack on Falwell based upon two premises. First, they claim that Falwell's supporters have roots in previous Christian anti-Semitic sects. Second, they claim that if Falwell and his followers are successful, there will be a merging of church and state in America that will have catastrophic consequences for the Jews. Each of these sophisms must be dealt with separately.

Jews in Israel and throughout the Diaspora have a well-founded historical memory of persecution by official bodies of both the Catholic and Protestant churches in Europe. We remember all too well the Spanish Inquisition, the anti-Semitic activities of Martin Luther, and the forced conversions of Jews in eastern Europe. In America itself, we recall the anti-Semitic diatribes of both Father Charles Coughlin and Gerald L. K. Smith, hurling calumny against both the Jews as a group and individual Jews as responsible for all the ills of American society.

It is the height of folly, however, to extrapolate from this the notion that every Christian political group is anti-Semitic. Nowhere in the sermons or writings of the leading spokesmen of the Fundamentalist Christian Right, including Jerry Falwell, Pat Robertson, etc., will you find any accusations that the Jews or Judaism are responsible for the ills of America.

You *will* find among the writings of such clergymen the assertion that Judaism is an incomplete religion because Jews do not acknowledge Jesus as the Messiah. As the late Nathan and Ruth Ann Perlmutter stated in their epic book, *The Real Anti-Semitism in America*, this is nothing more than a matter of religious conceit. Every religion has inherent in its dogma the notion that it is the only true and valid way to reach the Lord. For example, inherent in Judaism is the notion that Jesus is not divine, nor is he the Messiah. This is a religious conceit vis-a-vis Christianity that is only wrongful if Jews deny Christians anywhere the right and the freedom to practice their own religion. In fact, among sects of Judaism itself, there is a religious conceit regarding other Judaic branches. As the Perlmutters pointed out, a chief rabbi of Jerusalem has observed that God does not hear the *shofar* (ram's horn) when it is blown in a conservative synagogue on the High Holidays.

Furthermore, fundamentalist Protestants are not the only Christian clergymen voicing religious conceit. In 1987, Joseph Cardinal Ratzinger, the chief theologian of the Vatican, stated that a Jew encounters the full truth of his Judaism only by becoming a Catholic. Yet as noted by Rabbi Arthur Hertzberg (a Conservative Jewish rabbi, but a liberal in his politics) in an article written by him in the *New York Times* on December 22, 1987, "Judaism regards *itself* (italics are author's) as the principal heir and guardian of biblical truth."

Thus, religious conceit is only harmful—whether in Judaism or Christianity—when such religious conceit becomes religious intolerance. I have never heard Jerry Falwell indicate any contempt or intolerance for Judaism, in fact quite the reverse.

Yet even among liberal Jews who concede that Falwell and his followers are not anti-Semitic, there is a continuing argument that if Falwell's program is implemented, it will have disastrous consequences for American Jews.

Let me state at the outset that while I disagree significantly with Falwell on some issues, I hardly believe that the enactment of his proposals into law represents the death knell of American Jewish life.

As an example, take the issue of prayer in the public schools. While I oppose prayer in the public schools if such prayers are sectarian—that is to say, invoking the name of Jesus as a deity—I do not believe that non-sectarian prayers such as the old New York Regent's prayer have any real impact on our children in the public schools, positive or negative. Nor do I feel that displays of the nativity in public buildings are necessarily offensive, as long as they are not financed by the public treasury. The First Amendment of the Bill of Rights was never meant to preclude public display of religious preference by political leaders or the expression by government of a general belief in G-d* (such as the printing of the words "In G-d We Trust" on coins and currency). Rather, it was meant to prevent government from discriminating in favor of any *particular* religious denomination, as former Supreme Court Justice Potter Stewart pointed out in a number of key opinions.

As an American, I realize that I live in a nation where the overwhelming majority practices Christianity. I have no problem with the Christian majority in my nation having access to public places for the exercise of religion as long as I have the same rights.

Furthermore, I have no problem with our elected officials stressing their Christianity as a motivating force in their politics, as long as they do not express intolerance for my religion and people. I think that the

* In this book, the name of the Almighty is hyphenated in accordance with Jewish tradition.

reinstitution of Christian values in our society and culture, without any concomitant intolerance for Judaism, is exactly what Rev. Falwell is all about.

However, let us assume for the moment the very worst liberal distortion of Falwell's philosophy, i.e. let us assume that Falwell really means to reintroduce Christian prayers in our public schools. I was educated in a public school where Christian prayers and readings from the New Testament were recited every morning, and where Christmas pageants were given every year. While these prayers and pageants made me uncomfortable, they did not have any permanent deleterious impact on my life.

I think that on the agenda of American Jewish priorities, there are far more important priorities than the question of prayer in public schools. The greatest improvement in tolerance for American Jewry was brought about by the establishment of the State of Israel and the resulting increase in the respect for Jews not only in America but throughout the world. The issue of American support for the State of Israel is far more important to me than the issue of prayer in the public schools. On this issue, with whom do my liberal American Jewish friends feel more comfortable—the Rev. Falwell or the Revs. Jackson and Berrigan?

We Jews, as the Perlmutters stated, need all the friends we can get to support Israel in its struggle for survival. Many liberal Jews are concerned that the motivation of Falwell and other Christian fundamentalists is found in the New Testament prediction of a second coming. To such people, I can only respond with the Perlmutters' statement, "If the Messiah comes, on that very day we'll consider our options. Meanwhile, let's praise the Lord and pass the ammunition."

Chapter 6
The Liberals and Black Anti-Semitism

"Hymietown"
"I'm sick and tired of hearing about the Holocaust..."
"(Yasser Arafat is) educated, urbane, reasonable. I think his commitment to justice is an absolute one."
"We have the real obligation to separate Zionism from Judaism. Zionism is a kind of poisonous weed that is choking Judaism."
—The Collective Statements of Jesse Jackson

For me, this chapter is the most difficult and painful to write.

As a father, one of my highest priorities is to teach my son not to discriminate or hate anybody because of their race or creed. I am proud to see him make friends even at a young age with not only Americans of various races and creeds, but with children of immigrant Americans as well.

I am old enough to remember the glory days of the Black-Jewish alliance. Furthermore, as a member of the New Right, I am not hesitant to criticize the orthodoxies of the Old Right as symbolized by Barry Goldwater, who, although not a racist, often voted against legislation which legitimately insured to blacks rights which they had long been denied. I will readily admit that the old liberalism, as symbolized by Hubert Humphrey, had much to offer Black America. The old liberalism did have the negatives of welfarism and big government as described in Chapters 1 and 2, which actually hindered the progress of Black Americans. Nevertheless, the old liberalism must be credited with the passage of the Civil Rights Acts of 1964, 1965, and 1968, which properly legislated an end to discrimination in public accommodations, voting rights, and housing, respectively.

The new liberalism of the post-McGovern era offers Black Americans all the negatives of the old liberalism, together with few of its redeeming virtues. Among the new negatives of the new liberalism is affirmative action, a policy which attempts to guarantee equality of result rather than equality of opportunity, the latter being a legitimate goal for all Americans. Rather than being a godsend to Black Americans, affirmative action has actually resulted in White Americans questioning whether the professional achievements of individual Black Americans are due to merit or quota. This has a most devastating effect on the many Black Americans who have overcome numerous obstacles to achieve legitimate professional credentials and success, only to be doubted by Whites who believe such success and credentials to be achieved due to reverse discrimination.

The worst feature of the new liberalism, however, is its condonation of black anti-Semitism. This new doctrine reached its apogee in the 1984 presidential campaign of Jesse Jackson, where anti-Semitism was a salient feature in the same manner as white racism in the 1968 campaign of George Wallace.

The quotations at the beginning of this chapter are but a small sample of the anti-Semitic rhetoric of Jesse Jackson both before and during the 1984 presidential campaign. Jackson's course of conduct actually began with the 1979 firing of United Nations Ambassador Andrew Young (now Mayor of Atlanta), due to his contacts with PLO representatives at the United Nations, in violation of longstanding, bipartisan principles of American foreign policy prohibiting any contacts with the PLO.

Jackson and many left-wing black leaders viewed Young's firing as evidence of a malign, anti-black Jewish influence on American political affairs. In speech after speech, Jackson excoriated the Jewish community, in essence making the Jews a scapegoat for Black America. He increased his ties not only with the PLO, but also with the Arab League itself, which donated two separate checks for $100,000 to his organizations PUSH for Excellence and an affiliate, the PUSH Foundation. American Jews will never forget Jackson's alliance with Louis Farrakhan, who referred to Judaism as a "gutter religion," among his more mild comments. Yet Jackson absolutely refused to repudiate Farrakhan until the 1984 Democratic National Convention. Rather than appealing to the best impulses of the black community in the tradition of a Martin Luther King, Jr. or a Jackie Robinson, Jackson proved to be a master of demagoguery in appealing to the absolute worst impulse of the black body politic.

What disturbed me most, however, was not Jackson's anti-Semitic appeal but rather the absolute refusal of white liberals, including Jews, to repudiate him. Walter Mondale remained silent on Jackson well into the early spring of 1984. Liberal Jewish members of the House of Representatives and the Senate were almost uniformly silent. Perhaps most remarkable was the statement of Rabbi David Saperstein, a prominent liberal official of the Reform Jewish Union of American Hebrew Congregations who said in January 1984, "I think it would be a disaster if this turned into a Black-Jew confrontation... I believe Jesse Jackson has been trying to reach out to the Jewish community in the last several months and I would hate to see this reverse that process."

The message of Jewish liberals was clear: Special preferential treatment will be given to black anti-Semites.

Indeed, among Jewish and gentile liberals, there is an attempt to rationalize and distinguish black anti-Semitism as a natural outgrowth of economic conflict, as opposed to the anti-Semitism of other white ethnic groups, which, according to liberal dogma, simply resulted from ignorance and xenophobia. According to this liberal syllogism, the typical black ghetto resident comes into contact with four people who represent the white power establishment, to wit, the welfare worker, the teacher, the landlord, and the policeman. Three of these four representatives are Jewish, and the fourth, the policeman, is Irish. Thus, the argument continues, black anti-Semitism is a natural outgrowth of economic deprivation, given justifiable black resentment of the economic and educational structure and given the fact that three of the four representatives of this socio-economic structure are Jewish. Remove economic and educational discrimination against blacks, and black anti-Semitism will vanish.

This argument is not only silly, but also dangerous. Economic competition and deprivation may be used as a basis to rationalize not only black anti-Semitism but also the anti-Semitism of Polish, Russian, and Ukrainian peasants who took part in the pogroms of the 19th century. Indeed, many historians have attempted to explain the anti-Semitism of Adolf Hitler as that of an Austrian peasant who envied the Jews for their economic achievement in both Germany and the Austro-Hungarian empire. Whatever the roots of anti-Semitism, it can never be justified. In the case of Black anti-Semitism, it is true that the factors previously mentioned have created a climate in which anti-Semitism would flourish. It is both ridiculous and dangerous, however, to use the presence of Jews in the economic and educational social structure as a rationalization for black anti-Semitism, just as it is dangerous and ridiculous to use the high crime rate in the Black community as a justification for White racism. It is up to the responsible leadership in both the Jewish and black community to educate their followers that racism and bigotry are wrong and can never be condoned. And in this regard, it must be said that rather than appealing to his people for an end to anti-Semitism and promoting racial peace, in the tradition of Martin Luther King, Jr., Jesse Jackson instead appealed to the most base anti-Semitic trends in the Black community to rally support behind his presidential candidacy.

There is another argument for Jewish attempts to propitiate Jesse Jackson. This argument was best stated to me in a conversation I had with Rabbi Robert Gordis, one of the most prominent American Conservative Jewish rabbis in the 20th century and a man for whom I have the highest respect, notwithstanding his political liberalism. Gordis admitted to me that Jackson's appeal to black anti-Semitism was reprehensible. He told me, "Alan, while I agree with you on Jesse Jackson, we must remember that he does represent millions of blacks in America with whom we must live in peace." Thus, Rabbi Gordis asserted that in the interest of peace with the American Black Community, Jewish liberal forbearance in the face of Jackson's anti-Semitic appeal was justified.

At least this liberal argument acknowledges the evil inherent in Jackson's anti-Semitic appeal. It is a very dangerous precedent, however, to attempt to compound with Jackson on the basis that millions of blacks view him as their leader. The same argument could be made to justify negotiating with Yasser Arafat on the basis that millions of Palestinians view him as *their* leader. Jews have correctly refused to negotiate with Arafat in view of his terrorist activities. The fact that he enjoys widespread support among his people is no justification for dealing with him. Neither should the widespread support Jesse Jackson has among *his* people be any basis for refraining from responding to his blatant anti-Semitism.

Finally, Jewish liberals have consistently argued against giving Reverend Jerry Falwell a forum at Jewish events on the basis of their opposition to his views regarding religion and politics. Yet millions of American Evangelicals regard Rev. Falwell as their leader, and certainly we Jews must learn to live in peace with Evangelicals as well as blacks. If Jewish liberals are willing to accord Reverend Jackson respect on the basis that he is the leader of the black community, why then do they refuse to accord Reverend Falwell the same respect on the basis of his leadership of the Evangelical community? Such is the continuing paradox inherent in the liberal Jewish attitude toward Jesse Jackson.

*   *   *   *   *

Notwithstanding the rift between the Jewish and black communities accentuated by the Jackson candidacy, I remain hopeful that the Jewish-Black alliance can be reestablished.

To begin with, Jesse Jackson certainly is not the *only* American black leader. While I am a conservative, I acknowledge that there are many black liberals of the highest character, most notably Mayor Thomas Bradley of Los Angeles and former Representative Barbara Jordan. These people are living evidence that in order to obtain the allegiance of Black Americans, you do not have to appeal to blatant anti-Semitism à la Jesse Jackson.

It is also important for us Jews to realize that we certainly are not devoid of racism against Blacks in our own community. As a minor yet symbolic example, the word "schvartze," which originally in Yiddish only meant black, has come to have a most negative and derogatory connotation. We Jews must look in the mirror and ask no less of ourselves than we would ask of the black community in eliminating bigotry against any group.

Finally, as I have outlined in Chapter 3, supply side economics is the agenda that is of the highest economic benefit to both Jews and blacks. This new banner can readily be substituted for the old liberal banner under which Jews and blacks once both marched. As both blacks and Jews come to realize that it is free market economics which holds the key to progress for both communities, we will find our old alliance reborn and reinvigorated. When this happens, both blacks and Jews will look back with puzzlement on the 1980's, when anti-Semitism fueled a black presidential campaign and Jewish liberals remained silent.

Chapter 7
The Feminist Movement:
A Jewish Imperative?

"A woman of valor, who can find?"
—Proverbs, Chapter 31

The history of the Jewish people is replete with examples of notable achievement by women in roles traditionally reserved in other societies for men. From Deborah the judge who, together with Barak, led the Israelites triumphantly against the Caananite armies under Sisera to Golda Meir, Jewish women have successfully worn the mantle of leadership. Our people can indeed be proud of this accomplishment.

The post-1960 feminist movement has hardly been without impact upon the American Jewish community. In some respects, this impact has been salutary. Contemporary Jewish women could hardly be expected to be satisfied with the traditional stereotype of the Jewish mother making chicken soup for her husband and children, while the most important traditional religious roles were left to the male members of the family. I am both a Jewish Conservative and a Conservative Jew, and I welcome such changes in Conservative Jewish religious dogma, such as the entry of women into the Rabbinate, the occurrence of Bat Mitzvahs on Saturday morning, the granting of Aliot to women at Torah services, and the counting of women for a Minyan. All these changes should encourage the participation of women in religious ritual without in any way denigrating the concept of the traditional family.

Yet in many other ways, the post-1960 feminist movement poses serious practical and ethical problems for the American Jewish future. One of the real hidden "sleeper" issues is the Equal Rights Amendment.

At first glance, a fair-minded American Jew could hardly be expected to oppose the ERA. The ERA consists of a simple sentence which states "Equality of rights under the law shall not be abridged on account of sex." This seems altogether fair and simple; yet when one studies the practical implications of this amendment, one can envisage a scene of unbridled constitutional mischief.

The basic problem with ERA is that the area of sexual discrimination stands on a totally different footing from racial or religious discrimination. There is never any rational basis for racial or religious discrimination in any area of American public life, be it employment or government entitlement. There are, however, a number of areas where discrimination against sexual preference or actually in favor of a sex may be legitimate. For example, there is little sound or valid logic against the principle that only men should serve in combat and that husbands should have certain obligations of support of a wife and minor children. One could certainly find little fault with the notion that there should be Social Security benefits in favor of widows, while there is little compelling need for such benefits in favor of widowers. Furthermore, sexual preference certainly is a valid basis for discrimination against homosexual couples who may wish to adopt a child.

All these areas of sexual discrimination are totally legitimate and would be endangered by passage of the ERA. Judaism is definitely a moral, religious, and ethical system favoring a traditional concept of husband and wife as parents. There is absolutely no place in Judaism for allowance of homosexual couples as parents, and certainly observant Jews would be *compelled* to oppose any legislation such as the ERA that would preclude regulations prohibiting adoption by homosexual couples.

The problems with ERA, however, do not stop here. ERA poses a severe threat to the separation of church and state that liberals, particularly Jewish ones, so passionately embrace. I speak here of Orthodox rabbinical assemblies and Catholic monasteries, which, by religious doctrine, do not admit women to the clergy. Under ERA, such Orthodox rabbinical schools and Catholic seminaries would almost certainly lose their tax-exempt status.

Do Jews really wish to subscribe to such constitutional mischief? I hardly think so. While as a Conservative Jew I applaud the admission of women as rabbis, I certainly respect the doctrine sacred in the Orthodox Jewish interpretation of Halacha that women may never be admitted as Rabbis. I do not wish to provide a constitutional basis for a Jewish feminist to petition the Internal Revenue Service to have the Yeshiva University Rabbinical School lose its tax-exempt status on account of its non-admission of women.

The second key element of the post-1960 feminist movement is the support for continued legal status of abortion. My thoughts on this issue have been very heavily influenced by the book, *Marital Relations, Birth Control, and Abortion in Jewish Law*, by Rabbi David M. Feldman. Rabbi Feldman reviews the history of the development of Jewish law on this subject and concludes that under Jewish law, abortion is the taking of a potential life and not life itself. In the case of childbirth threatening the life of a mother, abortion is actually required as a matter of the mother's self-defense.

While abortion is not akin to homicide, it is indeed the taking of a potential life and under Jewish law should only be performed in order to save the mother from intense physical or emotional pain. Certainly, it is a very questionable moral and ethical practice.

I know numerous good and decent people who have had abortions, and I can hardly classify them as murderers. My own view on abortion is that while it is morally wrong, except where the life of the mother is at stake, it certainly is going to be performed in our society, whether or not it is legally mandated. And I would certainly prefer that such abortions be performed safely and legally in order to preserve the opportunities for mothers to have children in the future. If there is anything that Jewish law recognizes, it is that one cannot change human nature, and that rather than prohibiting outright questionable personal moral practices, they should be regulated so as to mitigate their most obnoxious consequences. Thus, in the Torah, rather than prohibiting slavery, which was very common at the time, Jewish law was designed to make slavery as humane as possible to preserve the physical and mental well being of the slaves.

Yet while I favor the continued legalization of abortion, I certainly feel strongly that it is a highly dubious moral practice. Anyone who has seen the film *The Silent Scream*, which shows an ultrasound of an abortion, has to view with horror what many feminist women have come to view as a practice involving a simple convenience for women. *The Silent Scream* was narrated by Dr. Bernard Nathanson, an atheist who at one time crusaded for legal abortion and ran New York State's first legal abortion clinic. Dr. Nathanson later totally renounced his prior views on abortion, stating that he now felt responsible for the murder of millions of babies.

What troubles me about the feminist movement is not its insistence on legal abortion but rather the way today's feminists totally ignore questions relating to the moral rights of the fetus. Anyone who believes in the moral and ethical principles of Judaism must give due consideration for the protection of the fetus. When Gloria Steinem lauds abortion as a matter of "reproductive freedom," traditional Jews have to be appalled. When other feminists defend abortion as a means of women controlling their own bodies, traditional Jews must realize that there is a total conflict between the values of the feminist movement and the high ethical standards of Judaism. Thus, the abortion issue displays again most graphically that the feminist movement is hardly a Jewish imperative.

*   *   *   *   *

The feminist movement is by no means a monolith. There are areas of disagreement among feminists as to the roles women should play in the traditional family unit. There is, however, a substantial strident element within the feminist movement that questions totally the traditional male-female familial roles. The traditional family is central to both the past and future of the Jewish people, and this new cultural feminist outlook certainly must be considered anathema to traditional Jews.

Gloria Steinem has often said that "A woman without a man is like a fish without a bicycle." It is one thing to say that a woman does not need to find her place and identity in life solely with reference to her mate. It is another thing to question the necessity for men and women to have a mate at all.

With the decline in birth rate and the ever growing number of divorces, the traditional American family is endangered, not just the Jewish family. The place of the family among Jewry, however, is absolutely crucial to our growth. This does not mean that a man or woman who remains single has no place in Jewish society. It is essential, however, for Jews to encourage successful marriages if our people are to remain a worldwide viable force.

Insofar as the feminist movement questions the necessity for marriage, it is hardly consistent with the Jewish agenda for the twentieth and twenty-first centuries. Within the family structure, there certainly is room for changing roles. Today, the working mother is not only an option, but often an economic necessity for the survival of the family. Certainly, however, it is a hope, and even a prayer, that Jewish families should continue to be formed, grow, and thrive.

*   *   *   *   *

In evaluating the political agenda of the post-1960 feminist movement, it is essential that Jews should evaluate the real political motives of the movement's most prominent organizations and leaders. As former White House liaison Faith Whittelsey told me at a December, 1983 conference at the White House, "The problem with the feminist movement isn't that it petitions for the advancement of the rights and interests of women as they see it. In this respect, the feminist movement is no different from any other special interest group. The *real* problem is that the feminist movement has a hidden agenda for liberal programs that have nothing at all to do with the rights and interests of women."

In this respect, one need only to examine the political endorsements of the National Organization for Women. This organization takes positions purportedly in the interest of women not only in matters such as ERA and abortion but also on national economic policy and foreign policy. Regardless of how strongly a person may have advocated ERA, abortion, or other liberal positions of special interest to women, the organization will turn its back on such a person and even oppose him or her if such a person is not sufficiently liberal in other areas. The organization's role as a purported defender of the interests of women is only a euphemistic shield for its hidden liberal political agenda.

The best example of this took place in the 1982 New Jersey U.S. Senatorial election. The Republican candidate was Millicent Fenwick who, as a four-term member of the U.S. House of Representatives had championed ardently and effectively the cause of ERA and legal abortion. Yet the organization endorsed her ultimately successful opponent, Frank Lautenberg, a man without any experience whatsoever in public political life, solely for the reason that Mrs. Fenwick had supported Ronald Reagan in some (but by no means all) matters of national economic and foreign policy.

It is clear that NOW was totally exposed as a fraud in this election. These self-anointed leaders of American women were simply using the cause of women as a front for their liberal agenda. Before Jews evaluate these post-1960 feminists, they would be wise to evaluate this feminist hidden agenda and find whether it is indeed compatible with the Jewish agenda. Certainly, as this chapter now shows, the feminist agenda is not a Jewish imperative.

Chapter 8
Democrats and Republicans:Who Gets the Ketubah?

"The Republican Party hereby explicitly repudiates hatred, big-otry, racism, or anti-semitism."
—Resolution sponsored by Senator Alfonse M. D'Amato adopted by Republican Party at 1984 Republican National Convention.

"We don't need such a resolution. We've been serving the best interests of the Jews."
—Representative Sam Gejdenson (D-Conn.), commenting on the CNN *Crossfire* show regarding his party's failure to adopt a similar resolution at the 1984 Democratic National Convention.

"How can I vote for a party that lets me be called 'Hymie' and my religion 'gutter'?"
"I am deeply troubled by what has happened to the Democratic Party. I have been closely associated with being a Democrat, but it is 1984 and I am afraid to vote Democratic. I am bewildered by what happened in San Francisco."
—Meshulam Riklis in an advertisement sponsored by him which appeared in the October 2, 1984 issues of the *Washington Post, New York Times,* and *Los Angeles Times.*

The Ketubah, the Jewish marriage covenant, is one of the most sacred documents in all of Judaism. This document spells out in detail the reciprocal obligations of a husband and wife. A breach of the Ketubah constitutes one of the most egregious sins in Judaism.

Since the election of Franklin Delano Roosevelt to the presidency in 1932, the American Jewish community has been the loyal loving wife in a Ketubah with the Democratic Party as husband. The problem is, however, that the Democratic Party husband cheats a hell of a lot on the Jewish community wife, and it is time for the American Jewish community to seek a Get, a Jewish bill of divorce.

The husband began to cheat very early in this marriage. The American Jewish community was lured into the Ketubah by President Roosevelt's promise to lift our country from the despair of the Depression. Actually, statistics show that the New Deal was a failure. The Great Depression was caused by Herbert Hoover's tax hike and the imposition of the Hawley-Smoot Tariff and not by a lack of social welfare programs. As late as 1939, the Great Depression was still ravaging America, and only the advent of the Second World War lifted the American economy from the Depression into unprecedented prosperity. Nevertheless, the American Jewish community, with its admirable concern for the poor, was seduced by Roosevelt's seeming concern with the little man.

When Hitler's Holocaust engulfed Europe, President Roosevelt did next to nothing to save as many Jews as possible from the Nazis. As has been documented in such books as *The Abandonment of the Jews* by David Wyman, and *While Six Million Died* by Arthur Morse, the insensitivity of the Roosevelt administration was absolutely appalling. Shiploads of Jews seeking refuge in the United States were refused entrance. American air power could have been used to bomb the rail lines to the concentration camps, but not a single such bomb was ever dropped. America refused to put any pressure on its British ally to open the gates of Palestine to Jewish escapees and, in fact, President Roosevelt met with King Ibn Saud of Saudi Arabia to assure him that the United States would not support the establishment of the Jewish state in Palestine after the war.

Nevertheless, the overwhelming majority of American Jews, supposedly the most highly educated block of American voters, blindly continued to support the Democratic Party. Many Jews felt vindicated on this score when President Harry Truman recognized the State of Israel immediately after its creation. Indeed, President Truman deserves great credit and gratitude for this. As the private papers of officials in the Truman administration show, however, this was hardly a gesture unmotivated by political concerns.

The private papers of former Secretary of Commerce, Agriculture and Vice President Henry Wallace are highly revealing in this regard. In 1946, Truman felt that Zionist lobbying for a Jewish state had exceeded reasonable bounds. In a cabinet meeting, he blurted out, "Jesus Christ couldn't please them 2000 years ago, how the hell am I supposed to please them now?"

Harry Truman, however, was no slouch as a politician. He knew that New York would be a vital state in his 1948 re-election campaign in which he was originally a decided underdog. This was a crucial factor in his decision to instruct the American Ambassador to the United Nations to vote for the partition of Palestine in November, 1947 and in his recognition of the State of Israel after its proclamation. It must be remembered, however, that the Truman administration hardly gave the State of Israel consistent unqualified support. Both Truman's Secretary of Defense James Forrestal and Dean Rusk, who served under Truman in the State Department and later became

John F. Kennedy's Secretary of State, fought vigorously against American support for the establishment of the new Jewish state. In March 1948, with the Jewish community in Palestine nearly strangled by the onslaught of Palestinian Arab guerrilla forces, the Truman administration delegation to the United Nations actually withdrew its support for the partition resolution creating the Jewish state and instead recommended the establishment of a U.N. trusteeship.

When the British evacuated Palestine and the State of Israel was proclaimed on May 14, 1948, President Truman did immediately extend recognition. One should remember, however, that the history of the Truman administration hardly was one of consistent unwaivering support for the Zionist cause.

Nevertheless, American Jewish liberals continued to espouse the notion that the Democratic Party was indeed the party of the Jews. They lent currency to this notion by pointing to the record of the Eisenhower administration in pressuring the Israelis to withdraw from the Sinai after the 1956 Sinai Campaign.

Indeed, one can strongly fault the Eisenhower administration for doing so. What everyone forgets, however, is that Eisenhower's Democratic opponent in the 1956 presidential election, Adlai E. Stevenson, the darling of the Jewish liberal salon set, also favored pressuring the Israelis to withdraw.

The American Jewish liberal community rejoiced at the election of John F. Kennedy over Richard M. Nixon in the 1960 presidential campaign. Yet the very first appointment John F. Kennedy made in the area of foreign policy was that of Dean Rusk as Secretary of State. This was the same anti-Zionist Dean Rusk who, in 1948 as Director of the State Department's Office of

Political Affairs, had attempted to persuade President Truman to commit American troops to Palestine in order to enforce a trusteeship plan against the will of the Jewish military forces. "If we did nothing" Rusk said, "it was likely that the Russians could and would take definite steps toward gaining control in Palestine through the infiltration of specially trained (Jewish) immigrants, or by otherwise capitalizing on the widespread violent civil war that would be likely to break out."

Thus, it was no surprise that the first two years of the Kennedy administration were highlighted by an active effort toward rapprochement with Gamal Abdul Nasser, the dictator of Egypt. This effort took the form of substantial economic assistance in an effort to lure Nasser away from Russian influence. The effort only was withdrawn when Nasser became involved in the civil war in Yemen against the Saudi Arabian supported royalist forces. At that point, the Kennedy administration felt it more vital to retain the friendship of the Saudis with their substantial oil reserves. Simultaneously, substantial sentiment against Kennedy administration policy mounted in the Congress, and the administration felt itself compelled to sell offensive weapons to Israel, including the Hawk ground-to-air missile.

The great irony in all this is that Lyndon Baines Johnson, the President who more than any other Democrat gave consistent unqualified support to the State of Israel, was the Democrat most reviled by Jewish liberals. In view of all this, one has to wonder at times whether American Jewish liberals are more loyal to their liberalism than to their Judaism.

Yet the most damning evidence rebutting the notion that the Democratic Party is the party for the Jews was yet to come in the Carter years.

Jimmy Carter devoted a substantial effort to wooing the American Jewish voters in 1976. He had to, for the Jewish vote would be absolutely necessary to his success in the Northeast, and these voters were highly suspicious of an Evangelist Democratic candidate from the Deep South.

One would have thought that Carter would refrain from making American policy in the Middle East an issue. The Nixon-Ford years, while not perfect, on the whole had been years in which the United States and Israel were more closely allied than ever before. American levels of economic and military assistance had reached new levels. In the Yom Kippur war of 1973, it was the American airlift of supplies directed by a President Nixon besieged by Watergate that resulted in the final Israeli victory. In fact, in 1976, Israeli Prime Minister Rabin stated that American-Israeli relations had never been better.

Yet Jimmy Carter had the audacity to attempt to woo Jewish voters with the argument that the Nixon-Ford administration had not been a true friend of Israel and that he, Jimmy Carter, would be a much more reliable ally. In sycophantic fashion, Carter roamed the country paying homage to every American Jewish organization he could find, pledging that "I'll never lie to you," and that America and Israel would be united as never before.

What followed was the most anti-Israeli administration in American history. This was the Carter administration of U.N. Ambassador Andrew Young who violated previous American-Israeli accords by direct contact with the PLO emissary to the United

Nations. This was an administration in which the U.S. Ambassador at the United Nations voted in a 1980 Security Council resolution to deny Israel authority over its holy city and capital, Jerusalem. This was an administration in which the President compared Yasser Arafat to the early leaders of the Black American Civil Rights Movement. This was a President whose brother had openly avowed friendship with the Libyan government and proclaimed, "There are a hell of a lot more Arabs than there are Jews." This was an administration which in every way sought to legitimize the PLO. In fact, after he left office, on the return home from the funeral of Egypt's President Sadat, Carter stated that the United States should negotiate with the PLO.

The Carter administration was even too much for many American Jewish liberals to stomach. While President Carter did have a plurality of the Jewish vote in his race against Ronald Reagan, he failed to carry a majority. The vote totals read: Carter, 45 percent; Reagan, 39 percent; Anderson, 16 percent. Yet given the egregious nature of the Carter administration, it is shocking that Jewish loyalty to the Democratic Party would result in vote totals as high as Carter achieved.

The worst was yet to come however, The 1984 Democratic National Convention and the preceding campaign represented an affront to any Jew, liberal or conservative, with any conscience about his people whatsoever.

As described in Chapter 6, the 1984 Democratic primary campaign witnessed the legitimization of anti-Semitism in the Democratic Party in the form of Jesse Jackson. Any fair-minded Democrat, Jew or gentile, could not help but be outraged by the repulsive anti-Semitism of Messrs. Jackson and Farrakhan. Enlightened Democrats sought to purge their party of this cancer.

One such delegate was Timothy F. Hagan of Ohio. He proposed a resolution in which the Democratic Party would officially condemn bigotry, racism, or anti-Semitism. The leadership of the Mondale campaign, however, refused to add this to the platform out of fear of offending Jackson and his supporters.

Thus, the final indignity was hurled against the loyal and loving Jewish wife by the unappreciative Democratic Party husband. Yet Congressman Gejdenson feels that the Democratic Party has the right to take the American Jewish community for granted, as he stated in the quotation I have outlined at the beginning of this chapter. To the American Jewish community, I can only say, in the words of former Governor Frank Clement of Tennessee, "How long, oh how long?"

I am not suggesting that the American Jewish community obtain a Get from the Democratic Party only to get a Ketubah with the Republican Party. The Republican record is hardly perfect. There have been Republican individuals such as former Representative Paul Findlay of Illinois and Senator Mark Hatfield of Oregon who openly back the Arab cause. Furthermore, there have been Democrats of liberal and conservative stripe who have been genuine friends of the American Jewish community, unmotivated by political considerations. Among such individuals I include the late Senators Henry Jackson of Washington and Frank Church of Idaho. These individuals represented states with small Jewish constituencies, yet they valiantly fought for the best interests of the State of Israel. What I am suggesting, however, is that when Jews give their loyalty solely to one political party, as they have to the Democratic Party, they will certainly be taken for granted. In answer to the question that is the title of this chapter, neither political party should get the Ketubah. Rather, the American Jewish community should force both the Democratic and Republican party suitors to actively compete for her favors and affection, and never again become a bride to be taken for granted.

Chapter 9
Anti-Semitism and the McCarthyism of the Left

"The commitment of modern conservatives to Israel is both theological and political...it does not matter if Israel and America have been brought together by cultural and political reasons, even without conscious choice...all that matters is reality. And today's reality calls for much more responsible American support for Israel...Israel's strength, with United States support, is at present the only real deterrent to Russian expansion in that vital part of the world."
—Former Interior Secretary James G. Watt in his book, *The Courage of a Conservative*, 1985.

"In order to get Treasury money for Israel (last year $3 billion) pro-Israel lobbyists must see to it that America's 'the Russians are coming' squads are in place so that they can continue to frighten the American people into spending enormous sums for 'defense' which also means the support of Israel in its never-ending wars against just about everyone...like most of our Israeli fifth columnists, Midge (Decter) isn't much interested in what the *goyim* were up to before Ellis Island...in the Middle East another predatory people (the Israelis) is busy stealing other people's land in the name of an alien theocracy. She (Midge Decter) is a propagandist for these predators (paid for ?) and that is what this nonsense is about...But now that we're really leveling with each other, I've got to tell you I don't much like your country, which is Israel."
—Gore Vidal, in an article entitled "The Empire Lovers Strike Back" appearing in the March 22, 1986 issue of *The Nation*.

The Jewish liberal establishment was in the vanguard of those who led the assault that culminated in the resignation of 1983 of James Watt as Interior Sec-

retary. He was accused of being anti-Semitic and
insensitive to handicapped people. Yet this was the
same Secretary of the Interior who had appeared as a
supporter at Israel Bond dinners in 1982 at a time
when Washington and Jerusalem were at odds over
Lebanon. This was the same James Watt who was a
strong vocal supporter of the establishment of a Holocaust Memorial in Washington D.C. This was the same
James Watt who gave lifetime passes to the handicapped for admittance into our National Parks.

Of Gore Vidal, who in the above quotation pro-
pounded some of the most inflammatory anti-Semitic
rhetoric in any American political journal during the
past fifty years, the Jewish liberal establishment said
nary a word.

The answer to this paradox is tragically simple.
James Watt is a victim and Gore Vidal is a beneficiary
of a new phenomenon which can best be labeled as
McCarthyism of the left, a political smear technique of
the left in which the words "anti-Semite" and "right
winger" are substituted as smear words for the old Joe
McCarthy opprobrium of "Communists." This conclu-
sion will disturb the thoughtful reader, but it is regret-
tably altogether too evident.

The chief proponents of Jewish liberalism cannot
help but be alarmed when they see liberalism as a
political force losing its grip on the Jewish community,
albeit too slowly for my satisfaction. The Jewish liberal
is terrified to see Ronald Reagan achieve Jewish vote
totals of thirty-nine and thirty-four percent respectively in the 1980 and 1984 elections. Even worse, he
can see that his arguments are starting to lose their
appeal among actively committed Jews. An active
Zionist anywhere who fears for Israeli survival against

Soviet encroachment will not be very impressed by arguments in favor of reducing America's defense budget. A struggling middle class Jewish family is not exactly going to be enchanted by a liberal economic theology that rewards idleness and punishes work by high taxes and more welfare programs. Young Jews struggling to enter into the job market will hardly be enthralled by the prospect of losing job opportunities due to affirmative action.

Therefore, when liberal arguments start to lose their persuasive force, Jewish liberals often try to appeal to age old fears of Jewish masses by labeling people on the political right as "anti-Semitic." This is exactly the equivalent of what Senator Joe McCarthy did in the 1950's by falsely labeling liberal dissenters as Communists. Like Senator Joe McCarthy, these Jewish McCarthyites of the left will take statements out of context and slips of the tongue to paint a false portrait of a political conservative as an anti-Semite. And never was there a more perfect victim of the McCarthyism of the Jewish left than James Watt.

Prior to his becoming Interior Secretary, James Watt was a life-long resident of the Rocky Mountain states. Thus, he strongly believed in conservation to preserve as much as possible the natural beauty of this region of the country. He believed, however, that conservation and the needs of the environment must be balanced with our domestic needs of development. As a key example, there was no sense in purchasing oil from the Arab states when we had oil on our own public lands available for extraction.

To liberals, particularly and paradoxically those residing on the East Coast, the Watt doctrine was heresy. These individuals were wedded to a policy of

no-growth resulting in part from an obsession to preserve in its natural state an area of the country which
these individuals hardly ever saw. Ironically, in the
Western and Rocky Mountain states, whose lands
were supposedly being plundered and despoiled by Mr.
Watt, his policies were overwhelmingly popular. The
people in this area of the country thirsted for balanced
development, and they understood the foolishness of
the liberal no-growth policy.

American Jews should have viewed James Watt as
a godsend. Here was a man whose goal was to reduce
American dependency on Arab oil. In this regard, Watt
actively sought cooperation of Israeli leaders, and as
we shall see, the Israelis were more than cooperative.
Among American Jews, however, instead of these
efforts being crowned with glory, in 1982 they were
grotesquely distorted by American Jewish liberals in
an effort to portray Watt as an anti-Semite.

During 1982, Watt formed a close relationship
with Israel's then Ambassador to the United States,
Moshe Arens. At a dinner during the 1982 Israeli
invasion of Lebanon, Arens expressed puzzlement to
Watt that the American Jewish community was not
more supportive of Watt's policy of selling leases to
drill for oil on the outer continental shelf. After the
dinner, Watt sent a letter to Arens summarizing their
discussions. I am reprinting this letter now in its
entirety, and I have italicized the portion that was
taken out of context by American Jewish liberals:

> "I appreciate the opportunity of dis-
> cussing with you the need for a strong,
> energy self-reliant America. If we do not
> reduce America's dependency upon for-

eign crude energy, there is a great risk that in future years America will be prevented from being the strong protector and friend of Israel that we are and want to be.

If the friends of Israel here in the United States really are concerned about the future of Israel, I believe they will aggressively support the Reagan Administration's efforts to develop the abundant energy wealth of America in a phased, orderly and environmentally sound way. *If the liberals of the Jewish community join with the other liberals of this Nation to oppose these efforts, they will weaken our ability to be a good friend of Israel. Your supporters in America need to know these facts.*

I look forward to opportunities to speak to groups of your supporters in this nation so that I might share with them the truth of what this administration is trying to do for America and the free world."

The meaning of this letter is clear to any child over the age of two. The Reagan administration intends to strongly support Israel. This support, however, will be hampered if the United States is reliant for energy on Arab oil. By opposing Reagan administration policies to make America energy self-sufficient, Jewish liberals are making America more reliant on Arab oil and thus less able to give the kind of support to Israel that the Reagan administration desires.

Instead of quoting this letter in its entirety, however, Jewish and gentile liberals took the italicized sentences out of context and claimed that Watt was threatening to withhold aid from Israel *in retaliation* for the opposition of American Jewish liberals to Reagan administration energy policies! Such a distortion was an act of ethical and moral disgrace. The assault on Watt was aided and abetted by two leading American Jewish Rabbinical liberals. Rabbi Alexander Schindler, the President of the Union of American Hebrew Congregations stated, "First of all, I don't like being appealed to as a Jew on an issue that is essentially of concern to all Americans." Rabbi David Saperstein, then head of the Interfaith Coalition on Energy said, "I find it politically and morally offensive. I hear a veiled threat that the Administration might cut back its support for Israel if Jewish Liberals do not remain quiet about energy policies, even if they think these policies are bad for America and bad for humankind." This is the same Rabbi Saperstein who, as I detailed earlier, went out of his way to propitiate one of Israel's arch-opponents, Jesse Jackson, yet smeared the character of one of its leading American supporters, James Watt.

Thankfully, Moshe Arens knew better. He and Watt became close friends. In fact, in 1985, Arens described Watt as "an outstanding American who has time and again proven his friendship for Israel." The Israeli government knew its true friends in America and would not be swayed by the McCarthyism of the Left practiced by Rabbis Saperstein and Schindler.

Unfortunately, among the American Jewish public, the anti-Watt liberals retained a wide following. Jim Watt would finally fall victim to the McCarthyism of the left in 1983 as he was impaled by his own slip of the tongue.

The incident bears recounting. In a September 1983 speech regarding the commission reviewing his coal-leasing policies, Watt stated, "We have ever kind of mix you can have. I have a black, I have a woman, two Jews, and a cripple. And we have talent."

Mr. Watt had a very clear message in this sentence. He was attempting to show that not even his liberal critics (who often insisted that people be appointed to positions on the basis of ethnicity rather than merit) could find fault with the ethnic balance of his Coal Commission. Had Mr. Watt used the phrase "handicapped person" or "disabled person" instead of "cripple," not even the most holier than thou liberal could have inferred any malice from his comments. Many individuals, however, view the word "cripple" as a pejorative term. To these individuals, the use of the word "cripple" denigrated physically-impaired Americans and other groups mentioned in that sentence.

Some physically-impaired Americans do not share this view. Take, for example the late Bill Veeck, former owner of the Chicago White Sox, Cleveland Indians, and St. Louis Browns baseball teams. One of Mr. Veeck's legs was amputated. In his book, *Veeck—As in Wreck*, the final chapter is entitled, "I'm Not Handicapped—I'm Crippled." In this chapter, Mr. Veeck states that he preferred the word "crippled" to "handicapped" since the word "handicapped" implies that a person cannot overcome his physical impairment.

Similar controversies have erupted whether one should call Afro-Americans "black" or "Negro." A person with Mr. Watt's political acumen and experience, however, should have avoided the use of the word "cripple" when he knew or should have known that his media critics would have a field day imputing malice to him. Persons in politics must be careful to avoid using phrases or words that may be distorted by their adversaries.

There are cases where the deliberate use of phrases displays grotesque bigotry that renders one unfit for public office. When Earl Butz told a tasteless joke that implied that blacks were oversexed and stupid, he was properly removed by President Gerald Ford as Agricultural Secretary. When Senator Jesse Helms stated that the Republican Party should concentrate on attracting white Southern Christian voters, one could properly have called him a racist and anti-Semite.

James Watt's remarks hardly fell into this category. As I have stated earlier in this chapter, there are few men in American public life who have been better friends of the Jewish community than James Watt. His record of support for the State of Israel and the Holocaust Memorial speaks for itself. Yet Mr. Watt was forced to leave office amidst a cascade from liberals alleging that he was an anti-Semite. Thus, the McCarthyism of the left had claimed its most prominent victim.

James Watt was not the actual target of the Jewish McCarthyites of the left, however. Ronald Reagan, himself, was. And when Reagan decided to visit the Bitburg Cemetery in 1985 which contained the remains of nearly two thousand Nazi soldiers, including forty-nine SS troops, these Jewish McCarthyites at long last thought they had their target within their sites.

Let me make it perfectly clear at the outset that I believe President Reagan's decision to visit Bitburg was a serious mistake for which I have no excuse. I thought it altogether proper that Eli Wiesel, Chairman of the United States Holocaust Memorial Council criticized the President severely for this mistaken decision. What I do object to most vigorously, however, was the way the Jewish McCarthyites of the left tried to use this mistake as grounds for asserting that the President was indifferent to the concerns and best interests of the American Jewish community. I can state unequivocally that American Jewry has never had a better friend in the White House than Ronald Reagan.

Morris B. Abram, the former president of the American Jewish Committee and a member of the United States Civil Rights Commission, put it best when he described the Bitburg visit as the "mistake of a friend—not the sin of an enemy" in a *New York Times* article entitled "Don't Be Misled by the Bitburg Trip" appearing Friday, May 10, 1985. As Mr. Abram pointed out, the degree of strategic cooperation between the United States and Israel has become closer than ever during the Reagan Administration, including participation in joint military exercises and the prepositioning of nonlethal equipment in Israel. As Abram further pointed out, during the Reagan Administration, Israel became the first United States trading partner to be given fully free access to American markets. It was the Reagan administration that organized the airlift of Ethiopian Jews to Israel by the dispatch of United States Air Force planes to the Sudan. As for the Reagan administration's record on Soviet Jews, I would quote Mr. Abram from the same article, "By all accounts that I have heard—and I have been privy to many here and in Israel—no previous administration has been as steadfast or as forceful as this one in supporting the cause of Soviet Jews." And as Abram further pointed out, "Eli Wiesel, himself, while criticizing Reagan for the Bitburg visit, credited the President for having been brought to tears at the remembrance of Nazi atrocities against the Jews." One could expect, however, such fairness from Mr. Wiesel who acted out of principle and not out of base political motives. One could not expect such fairness from the Jewish McCarthyites of the left who used President Reagan's Bitburg misjudgment as the centerpiece of their *ad hominem* attack against his character and sensitivity to the Jewish community. These same Jewish McCarthyites of the left were silent regarding the behavior of his predecessor, Jimmy Carter, who once compared Yasser Arafat and the PLO with the moderates of the Civil Rights movement of the 1960's. Such a double standard is McCarthyism, plain and simple.

This double standard was never more evident than by the silence of the Jewish liberal left in the face of Gore Vidal's inflammatory anti-Semitic rhetoric described at the beginning of this chapter.

The same Jewish liberals who tried to characterize James Watt and Ronald Reagan as anti-Semites remained almost totally silent in the case of Mr. Vidal. Norman Podhoretz, the editor of *Commentary* magazine, attempted to have thirty prominent friends of *The Nation* disavow Vidal's article, and only six did so.

This refusal is absolutely frightening. It seems to signal that both Jewish and gentile liberals will ignore genuine anti-Semitism of the left while at the same time attempting to smear conservatives like Reagan and Watt as anti-Semites.

In the 1950's, Senator Joe McCarthy spent so much

time falsely slandering liberals as Communists that you hardly knew when you saw a genuine Communist. Today's Jewish liberals are likewise trying to characterize conservatives as anti-Semites. And as we saw in the cases of Reagan and Watt, sometimes this calumny misfires and only serves to hurt conservative figures who have been genuine friends of the Jewish community. The charge of anti-Semitism is a serious one, and it should not be debased by today's Jewish McCarthyites of the left as a convenient political smear tactic for the dying American liberal movement.

Chapter 10
1986—The Jewish Democrat Ketubah Is Renewed

"In reality, more than any ethnic group, the Jews elected a Democratic Senate in the 1986 election."
—Anonymous Washington political consultant in conversation with the author

The Ketubah between American Jewry and the Democratic Party of which I wrote in Chapter 8 was grounded on a philosophical basis of adherence to liberalism. However misguided that philosophy might be, at least it was a marriage based upon a shared ideological value. The 1985 and 1986 elections suggest a new, more astounding development: a Ketubah based upon an almost blind loyalty to the Democratic Party label per se that cannot be explained in terms of ideological orientation.

Nineteen Eighty-five was the year that Jewish New Jerseyans rejected the most liberal Republican statewide office holder in the country, despite his attraction of almost every other New Jersey ethnic group. In 1986, American Jewry played an astoundingly pivotal role in electing a Democratic U.S. Senate despite the incumbency of a Republican administration and Senate that had been extremely supportive of the State of Israel. These two developments displayed most graphically that American Jewish loyalties to the Democratic Party may well endure, despite changes in philosophy on the part of either party. For a people regarded as being especially issue oriented and well informed, such blind loyalty to a party label is most distressing.

*   *   *   *   *

I first met New Jersey Governor Thomas Kean in 1977 when he was initially seeking the Republican nomination for Governor. I worked diligently for one of his conservative Republican opponents in the 1981 Republican primary. Since he took office in 1982, I have written articles and letters in opposition to many of his policies.

To put it bluntly, Tom Kean is not my kind of Republican. He is, in fact, the most liberal Republican to appear on the national scene in the past 25 years; even more liberal than former Representative and presidential candidate, John Anderson. He actively opposed the candidacies of Barry Goldwater and Ronald Reagan in 1964 and 1976 respectively. He was an early advocate for a substantial reduction in President Reagan's defense budget and for the firing of James Watt. He was one of only three Republican governors at the 1984 Governor's conference who supported a Democratic resolution to reduce the deficit by an increase in taxes. As governor, he has raised the State income taxes to the highest level in history and has supported annual budget increases well above the rate of inflation. He has supported wetland measures greatly impacting private property owners. In 1985, he signed a bill outlawing New Jersey treasury investments in South Africa that Bella Abzug and Amy Carter would have applauded. He is one of those rare Republicans who has supported the nuclear freeze movement.

In summary, Tom Kean is a Republican in name only who would be more at home with the broad mainstream of the Democratic party. I must confess, however, that I do have a soft spot for Tom Kean. Few American political families have been more supportive and sensitive to Jewish causes than the Kean family and Tom Kean has carried on ths laudable tradition.

Tom Kean's father Robert was a member of the U.S. House of Representatives in the Roosevelt-Truman era. During the Holocaust, he was one of those rare Republicans who castigated the Roosevelt administration for not taking more vigorous measures to stop the genocide of European Jewry. In spite of possible negative political repercussions, he advocated opening the gates of America for Jewish refugees escaping the Holocaust. After the war, he fought vigorously for the establishment of the State of Israel.

There is no doubt that Tom Kean has carried on this tradition. He has vigorously championed the State of Israel and the movement to put the Holocaust into the curriculum of our public schools. He has sponsored measures to deal severely with anti-Semitic vandals defacing New Jersey synagogues and other Jewish institutions. He certainly has earned and deserves the support of Jews in elections.

In spite of his liberalism and his support for the Jewish causes, however, Tom Kean could not break the spell of the Democratic label in 1985. In the 1985 election, Tom Kean won the highest landslide in the history of New Jersey. He even carried the black community, which has virtually never supported any Republican, black or white, in any statewide election during the last three decades. He received support of liberal environmental groups and the media.

Only one ethnic group failed to give Tom Kean a majority—the Jews!

There have been many explanations for this, the most obvious being the fact that Kean's opponent, former Essex County executive, Peter Shapiro, is Jewish. This explanation, however, is totally invalid.

If there is any ethnic group that does not consist of "homers", it is the Jews. In both primary and general elections, Jewish voters have rejected members of their own ethnic group in favor of other candidates. In his book *Ethnic America*, the eminent economist Thomas Sowell illustrates two strong examples. In 1939, a liberal Democrat, Robert Wagner, Sr., won the election and support of the Jewish community in his race for the U.S. Senate in the State of New York against a Jewish opponent. In 1962, U.S. Senator Jacob Javits (R-N.Y.) won a landslide re-election against his opponent, Democrat James Donovan; yet Javits, an acknowledged champion of the causes of his own Jewish people, lost the Jewish vote to Donovan.

The evidence seems to prove a disturbing notion; that loyalty of American Jewry to the Democratic party per se is even stronger than their loyalty to liberalism. In the case of Tom Kean, one sees a politician who satisfied every litmus test of liberalism and still failed to win the support of the Jewish community, simply because he had the wrong party label. Such thoughtless attachment to a label is unbecoming to one of America's most highly educated and successful ethnic groups.

Yet in 1986, there was no sign that the Democratic party "hechscher" was losing its credibility among

American Jews. In fact, in 1986, financial assistance from American pro-Israel political action committees played a most pivotal role in the election of a Democratic U.S. Senate.

In articles appearing in the *Wall Street Journal* on June 24, 1987 and the *New York Times* on July 7, 1987, the role of pro-Israel political action committees in the 1986 Congressional elections was described in depth. The following chart appeared in the *Times* article showing contributions by the pro-Israel political action committees:

Senate

Thomas A. Daschle, D-S.D.	$ 200,280
Alan Cranston, D-Calif.	182,982
John V. Evans, D-Idaho	166,500
Arlen Specter, R-Pa.	135,773
Harry M. Reid, D-Nev.	130,540
Robert W. Kasten, Jr., R-Wis.	104,350
Timothy E. Wirth, D-Colo.	80,500
Patrick J. Leahy, D-Vt.	79,200
Harriet Woods, D-Mo.	77,800
Paula Hawkins, R-Fla.	76,950
Wyche Fowler, Jr., D-Ga.	74,100
Terry Sanford, D-N.C.	70,750
John McCain, R-Ariz.	45,500
James R. Jones, D-Okla.	44,000
Daniel K. Inouye, D-Hawaii	43,975

House

Edward F. Feighan, D-Ohio	$ 46,750
Larry Smith, D-Fla.	46,050
Vin Weber, R-Minn.	34,700
Sam Gejdenson, D-Conn.	31,579
Howard E. Wolpe, D-Mich.	30,500
Bob Carr, D-Mich.	28,250
Peter H. Kostmayer, D-Pa.	26,000
David R. Obey, D-Wisc.	24,250
Cardiss Collins, D-Ill.	21,000
Mel Levine, D-Calif.	18,500
Les AuCoin, D-Ore.	17,500
Tim Johnson, D-S.D.	15,750
James Jontz, D-Ind.	15,500
John R. Lewis, D-Ga.	15,250
Dante B. Fascell, D-Fla.	15,000

One will note the preponderance of Democratic Party recipients, notwithstanding the fact that the Republican Senate was most sympathetic and supportive of Israel during the years 1981 through 1986. In the cases of Tom Daschle and Alan Cranston, support for such Democrats was understandable in view of the questionable records on Israel of their Republican opponents. In other cases, however, such support for Democrats appears ludicrous.

In the case of Timothy Wirth, his opponent, Ken Kramer, had an outstanding record on Israel in the House of Representatives. His view of a strong U.S. Defense budget, as compared to that of Wirth, was far more in Israel's interest. Yet the pro-Israel PACs gave Wirth their support.

Consider the case of Harriet Woods. Her successful

opponent, Christopher "Kit" Bond, was an outstanding candidate from every Jewish perspective. As Governor of Missouri, he maintained very close relations
with the Jewish community and actively travelled to
Israel in order to study its problems. While Harriet
Woods herself is Jewish, in what appeared to be an
attempt to woo farmers (who may have not realized
that Ms. Woods was Jewish), she castigated "East
Coast Collection Agencies" and "New York Banks,"
identical terms used by anti-Semitic groups that
sought to incite anti-Semitism in the farm community.
In view of such disgraceful campaign tactics, Jewish
financial support of Ms. Woods bordered on political
obscenity.

In the House races, one finds only one Republican
among the top 15 recipients of pro-Israel political
action committees, to wit, Vin Weber. Among these top
15 is Peter Kostmayer, who has been an outspoken
opponent of assistance to the freedom fighters seeking
to overthrow the Sandinistas in Nicaragua, the most
anti-Semitic regime in the history of the Western
Hemisphere. Yet while Kostmayer was garnering
Jewish financial support, such pro-Israel Republican
stalwarts as New Jersey's Jim Courter, New York's
Jack Kemp, and Georgia's Newt Gingrich failed to
make the list.

Ultimately, such one-party bias may turn out to be
very counter-productive. If Republicans feel that regardless of their record on Jewish issues they still will
not obtain Jewish political support, they may well tend
to be less sensitive to Jewish concerns. If Democrats
feel secure in the knowledge that they will obtain
Jewish support against their Republican opponents,
regardless of the issues involved, they may take the

Jewish vote for granted and feel secure in making concessions to pro-Arab groups as well. Thus, Jewish blind financial support to Democratic candidates may result in a lesser Jewish influence in both Republican and Democratic parties.

There is a passage in the Siddur (the Jewish prayer book) which states, "it is better to trust in G-d than to trust in princes." Perhaps one might add the passage, "it is better to trust in political philosophy than in party labels." Unfortunately, the American Jewish community seems to think at times that there is an eleventh commandment, "Thou shall vote Democrat, regardless of the opponent." Such a Mitzvah, however, was not ordained at Mt. Sinai.

Chapter 11
Judaism and Judicial Activism:
The Bork Controversy

"And all this word shall I command you that ye shall observe to do;
Thou shalt not add thereto nor diminish from it."
—Deuteronomy 13–1

The rejection by the United States Senate of President Reagan's nomination of Robert Bork to the Supreme Court was for me a personal tragedy, not only as an attorney and as an American political conservative, but also as an American Jew.

As an attorney I was appalled by the conduct of the Senate hearings that even surpassed the McCarthy hearings in their slanderous treatment of the principal witness, in this case Judge Bork. In the words of Pat Buchanan, Bork was the most qualified judge appointed to the court since Felix Frankfurter. He had distinguished himself as a U.S. Solicitor General, as a professor at Yale and finally as a judge on the District of Columbia Court of Appeals.

Judge Bork, however, was much more than a resume. In his personal life and career, he had by deeds and not by mere words demonstrated his personal commitment to the elimination of racial and ethnic prejudice. Early in his career, in 1957, as a junior associate in a Chicago law firm, he fought for and won employment for a lawyer, Howard Krane, whom the firm's management did not want to hire because he

was Jewish. As Solicitor General, he supported a black
female lawyer in the Justice Department, Jewel
Lafontant, who complained that she was excluded
from meetings by her white male colleagues. As a
Federal Judge, he voted in favor of 1) female flight
attendants at Northwest Airlines who suffered pay
discrimination; 2) female foreign service officers at the
State Department who believed they had been subject
to discrimination in pay and promotion; 3) a Naval
Officer who claimed he had been passed over for
promotion because he was black.

In view of this record, how does one explain Ted
Kennedy's following statement at the time of Robert
Bork's nomination?

> Robert Bork's America is a land in which
> women would be forced into back alley
> abortions, blacks would sit at segregated
> lunch counters, rogue police could break
> down citizen's doors in midnight raids and
> the doors of Federal Courts would be shut
> on millions of citizens.

The revulsion of Senator Kennedy and his
soulmates in People for the American Way, National
Organization for Women, etc. was best explained
unwittingly by former Carter administration official,
Hodding Carter, who explained in a *Wall Street Journal* article that the Bork nomination:

> requires liberals like me to confront a
> reality we don't really want to confront,
> which is that we are dependent to a large
> part on the least democratic institution
> (the Supreme Court) to define what it is we
> are no longer able to find out there in the
> electorate.

The message is clear: The liberals have been rejected at the polling place, and therefore, they are no longer able to impose their agenda on the American public. Instead, they will rely upon the unelected Supreme Court to enact their agenda.

This is exactly what the framers of our Constitution guarded against in drafting Article III of the Constitution. They believed that the functions of the judiciary should be limited to interpreting statutes for their compliance with the Constitution and *not* to enact new laws. They realized that a judiciary which viewed itself as having the latter power would have the ability to function almost as an unelected legislature, without any accountability to the voters. In Federalist Paper No. 81, Alexander Hamilton envisioned that the judiciary would be the weakest branch of the government, since in his words, it would have no sword nor purse. Accordingly, he deemed it absolutely necessary that its judgments be respected; nevertheless, if the Supreme Court went beyond its explicitly granted powers and infringed upon the prerogatives of the legislature or executive, impeachment of such infringing judges would be the appropriate remedy.

In this era, impeachment carries with it a horrible stigma, and therefore, I would not advocate impeachment as the proper way to deal with honorable judges, who in good faith, due to faulty interpretation of the Constitution, illegitimately infringed upon powers granted to the other branches of government. The need is for the appointment of *new* judges who will strictly interpret statutes and actions of the executive branch in terms of their compliance with the language of the Constitution and will *not* base their decisions on their own personal values, disregarding the Constitution's provisions.

It should also be noted that such a strict con-
structionist approach does not automatically mean a
total majoritarian approach to issues of minority
rights. Minority rights are guaranteed by the
Constitution itself, specifically, in 1) its first ten
amendments, known as the Bill of Rights, 2) the thir-
teenth, fourteenth, and fifteenth amendments, which
include the abolition of slavery, the Equal Protection of
the Laws clause, and the guarantee of voting rights to
all citizens, and 3) the nineteenth amendment, which
guarantees suffrage regardless of sex. The Court must
outlaw all measures which run afoul of these amendments, such as racial segregation in schools, which
was declared unconstitutional in the *Brown v. Board
of Education* case. In that case, the Supreme Court
nobly performed its task of outlawing measures which
infringe upon the Constitutional protection of
minorities.

But it is a wholly different matter, however, when
the Supreme Court creates new "rights" which do not
appear in the Constitution and which may, in fact,
involve the licensing of activities harmful to the community at large.

I speak particularly of the Supreme Court's decision in *Griswold v. Connecticut* (which outlawed a
Connecticut statute forbidding the dispensing of birth
control pills) and in *Rowe v. Wade* (which forbade
states from outlawing abortions during the first six
months of pregnancy). Like Robert Bork, I too believe
that the Connecticut statute on birth control pills was,
in his words, "nutty." I also, at the risk of censure from
my conservative friends, believe that abortion should
be legal. I feel most strongly, however, that the way to
repeal the Connecticut statute and to legalize abortion

was through legislative action at either the State or Federal level and not through what Judge Bork defined as "judicial ukase." These two cases stemmed from the notion of an unlimited "right of personal privacy." The establishment of this "right" may well create societal havoc.

To be sure, the amendments to the Constitution establish certain spheres of personal privacy, such as in the Fourth Amendment (which protects the privacy of one's person, papers, and property), the First Amendment (which protects one's right of privacy in his religious observance and speech), the Second Amendment (which *explicitly* protects one's right to privately bear arms for protection of his home and property, although liberals have blindly refused to recognize the literal language of the Constitution in this regard), and the Ninth Amendment (which grants State legislatures the power to pass new legislation expanding one's zone of personal privacy).

In all these cases, the Constitution explicitly protects certain spheres of personal privacy. The *Griswold* case, however, establishes an *unlimited* right of personal privacy which is never explicitly spelled out in the Constitution or any statute.

Where does such an unlimited right of privacy begin and where does it end? Does it mean that one is free to utilize hallucinogenic drugs in his own home? Does it mean that boards of health may never enter into a home where grossly unsanitary practices are taking place, since they only involve the consenting tenants? Does it mean that universities founded on certain religious bases must recognize homosexual student organizations because to not do so would be a violation of the private rights of homosexuals? Does it

mean that zoning laws are unconstitutional because
they violate the property owner's free and unfettered
rights of privacy to use his property as he sees fit?

It is clear on its face that such a judicially enacted
measure has the potential of playing havoc with our
system of well-ordered liberty. Even the liberal Justice
Hugo Black recognized this in dissenting from the
majority in the *Griswold* decision. Yet this new free
and unfettered privacy right was expanded even further in the *Rowe v. Wade* decision, as the Supreme
Court found that statutes enacted by State legislatures outlawing abortion within the first six months of
pregnancy violated the rights of privacy of women.

What makes the *Rowe v. Wade* case even more
frightening is that the judges arbitrarily established
as law their values regarding the status of the fetus in
stating that it was only entitled to protection after the
sixth month of pregnancy. Nowhere in the
Constitution is such a power of legislating a definition
of life granted to the Supreme Court. The Court's
decision in the *Rowe v. Wade* case constituted an act of
legislation, which is strictly within the purview of
state legislatures and the Congress.

For the Jewish community, this new free and
unfettered right of privacy, which is *nowhere stated in
the Constitution*, represents a possible infringement
on the free and unfettered practice of Judaism in
Jewish institutions, which *is explicitly protected* by the
First Amendment. A few examples suffice in this
regard.

Will this Court-legislated right of privacy preclude
Yeshiva University from outlawing on-campus homosexual student associations, whose presence would
violate the law of the Torah, upon which this religious
institution is grounded?

Will this new right of privacy require federally supported Jewish hospitals to perform abortions, albeit that such abortions violate Jewish law?

And will this new right of privacy affect a Jewish woman's ability to compel her husband to give her a "Get," a Jewish bill of divorce? I speak of the New York statute which compels a husband to remove all barriers to the wife's remarriage. This statute compels a recalcitrant Jewish husband to give his wife a "Get" in order that she may remarry. Such legislation, however, may be declared to be unconstitutional, in that it violates a husband's *Griswold* unfettered right of privacy, which would entitle him to refuse to take part in a religious ceremony if he wished. What would prevent a court from applying *Griswold* in such a manner? How ironic it would be if such a liberal inspired, judicially legislated right of privacy resulted in agony for Jewish women whom liberals supposedly would want to protect!

The constitutional mischief of *Griswold* resulted from the notion that judges may utilize their own personal values in "legislating" new "rights." Two of the finest Supreme Court justices in history, Louis Brandeis and Felix Frankfurter, both warned against the Supreme Court assuming the character of superlegislature and imposing their personal views in deciding the constitutionality of a law. Both of these gentlemen were considered to be liberals; however, unlike many liberal jurists today, they realized that we have a government of laws and not of men and as such they did not have the right to substitute their personal views for the language in the Constitution.

Many readers may feel that my examples of possible extensions of the *Griswold* right of privacy are extreme and that no responsible court would ever interpret a right of privacy as such. Yet once you give unelected men the free and unfettered right to impose their personal values in enacting new "rights" and to interpret them uninhibited by the literal language of the Constitution, who can foretell where such interpretations will lead? As an example, who could have predicted in 1954 that the laudable decision in *Brown v. Board of Education* would someday be interpreted as requiring busing to achieve racial balance?

In order to guard against judicial imperialism and the establishment of the Supreme Court as an unelected super legislature, it is absolutely necessary to appoint strict constructionists who will feel themselves bound by the language of the Constitution and not free to impose their own personal agenda. In short, we need judges to act in the tradition of a Brandeis and a Frankfurter. Robert Bork was very much in this tradition. In fact, there were very definite historical parallels between Brandeis and Bork. Like Brandeis, Bork was opposed by various presidents of the American Bar Association. Like Brandeis, Bork was denounced by leading media institutions, such as the *New York Times*. Unlike in the Brandeis appointment, however, the opponents of Bork were able to utilize television in spreading their smear campaign, and thus the Supreme Court was deprived of a man who may well have been one of its greatest justices.

For the Jewish community, the Bork nomination was characterized by two other notable aspects: 1) the efforts of liberal secular Jewish institutions to persuade the U.S. Senate that the Jewish community monolithically opposed Bork; and 2) the unethical efforts of the office of Senator Howard Metzenbaum to intimidate a black supporter of Bork from testifying, said unethical activities which, when combined with previous unethical practices of Senator Metzenbaum, one of the U.S. Senate's most highly publicized Jewish members, constituted a severe embarrassment to the Jewish community.

The American Jewish community response to President Reagan's nomination of Judge Robert Bork to the Supreme Court was highly predictable.

The American Jewish Congress, perhaps the leading American Jewish liberal organization, not surprisingly, issued a statement opposing the nomination. In this statement, issued by Theodore R. Mann, the president, the organization objected to Bork's disagreement with "a long series of significant precedents which are now deeply embedded in American law which have significantly expanded the rights of citizens with respect to such crucial areas as privacy, free speech, civil rights and church-state separation."

The logic of this statement is rather amusing. Mr. Mann says that any efforts to overturn precedents embedded in American law on these issues would be "a radical step." I wonder if Mr. Mann would consider as "radicals" those judges who would have opposed such "deeply embedded precedents" as the Dred Scott decision of 1858 legitimizing slavery and the nineteenth-century *Plessy v. Ferguson* decision which held racially segregated schools to be constitutional. By Mr. Mann's logic, the Warren Court must be considered to be radical for 1) overturning the *Plessy v. Ferguson* decision, 2) its one-man-one-vote decision which outlawed the "deeply embedded" American tradition of State Senates apportioned on the basis of areas and not population, and 3) various decisions which vitiated the test enunciated by former Justice Oliver Wendell Holmes limiting speech constituting a "clear and present danger" by its incitement of violence.

The hypocrisy in Mr. Mann's statement is transparent. Mr. Mann really does not object to the overturning of precedents which he considers erroneous. It is only when a judge advocates rulings that overturn precedents near and dear to Mr. Mann's heart that such a judge becomes a radical!

Thankfully, however, the views of the American Jewish Congress were not the only views expressed on the Bork nomination.

The *Jewish Press*, the largest independent Anglo-Jewish weekly newspaper, supported the Bork nomination in its issue of Friday, September 11, 1987. It described the Bork nomination as "a matter of life and death for ourselves, our children and our grandchildren. Most of the unchecked violent crime, including street muggings, rapes, burglaries, etc., and the breakdown of our criminal justice system—are largely due to soft-on-crime, radical liberal judges on the Supreme Court and lower courts." The *Jewish Press* lauded Bork for his service on the U.S. Court of Appeals in the District of Columbia, commending his rulings in favor of the death penalty and his rejection of the appeal of Nazi war criminal, Ivan Demjanjuk, seeking to avoid deportation to Israel. The editorial pointed out that Bork had opposed job quotas, which discriminate against Jews and other whites seeking employment. Furthermore, the editorial praised Bork for his stance against the attempts of "an activist liberal judiciary imposing the homosexual lifestyle ('Gay Rights') agenda on the American people, including our young school children."

Yet, if you followed coverage in the secular press, you would be far more likely to read the statements of the American Jewish Congress than the endorsement of the *Jewish Press*. In short, the non-Jewish community had the impression that Jewish opposition to Bork was monolithic. It was for this exact reason that Rabbi William Handler of the Union of Orthodox Rabbis of the United States arranged to testify in favor of Bork before the Senate Judiciary Committee.

The Union is the oldest rabbinical organization in the United States. It represents 600 rabbis and heads of seminaries. According to Rabbi Handler, as stated in an article written by journalist Ray Kerrison in the *New York Post* on October 22, 1987 "We (the Union) endorsed Judge Bork precisely for the reasons that the secular organizations opposed him on the issues of recognition of G-d, abortion, and gay rights."

Thus, in spite of the efforts of the American Jewish Congress, thankfully there are Rabbi Handlers to contest the view that judicial liberalism is the authentic philosophy of the Jewish community. Yet if one reads the excellent Kerrison article, one may well infer from the Rabbi's comments that Senator Joseph Biden's aide, Dianne Huffman, actually tried to keep his view from being heard. This attempt, according to Rabbi Handler, was "part of an orchestrated plan to selectively keep pro-Bork witnesses from testifying."

According to Rabbi Handler, Huffman called the executive director of the Union the day before Rabbi Handler's scheduled appearance to say that it had been cancelled. On that same date, however, he had received a call from the office of Senator Strom Thurmond (R-So. Carolina) advising him when and where to appear.

Rabbi Handler went to Washington anyway and discovered his appearance had not been cancelled. He was livid and went before the Committee, accusing Biden of attempting to censor the Orthodox Jewish view. Although Biden advised the Rabbi that the cancellation was a mistake, Handler remains unconvinced, especially in view of statements made to another scheduled pro-Bork witness, a black professor at the Indiana Law School, John T. Baker, by Linda Greene, an aide to Senator Howard Metzenbaum. In order to evaluate Rabbi Handler's charge, it is appropriate to review the statements made by Linda Greene and the activities of her boss, Howard Metzenbaum.

Senator Metzenbaum was one of a featured quartet of senators who may well be labeled as the Democratic gang of "Four Ethical Charlatans." Rounding out the quartet were Senators Biden, Edward Kennedy of Massachusetts, and Patrick Leahy of Vermont. These four individuals, in a grossly sanctimonious fashion, led the efforts of the majority on the Senate Judiciary Committee to smear the character and reputation of Robert Bork: however, these individuals proved the classic truism that people who live in glass houses shouldn't throw stones at other people's windows.

Their assault on Bork was so venomous that Mayor Edward I. Koch of New York City, himself a Democrat, felt compelled to say that Bork had been "horribly mistreated" during the Senate Judiciary Committee hearings. According to Koch, the chief culprits were Biden and Kennedy. Koch stated, "To have Joe Biden and Ted Kennedy lecture on morality is a sin. Some of the things they have done (during the three weeks of hearings) have hurt the body politic."

Indeed, Koch may have understated the degree of ethical hypocrisy of the Democratic majority on the Senate Judiciary Committee, especially when one scrutinizes at close range the Four Ethical Charlatans.

First, there was Senator Edward M. Kennedy, the hero of Chappaquiddick. A gentleman whose ethics were so high that he left a woman in his car in the water overnight, conferring with top aides before he reported the drowning to the police. A man who accused Robert Bork of being a threat to the Bill of Rights, while within a few months after Bork was denied confirmation, he would conduct what Ed Koch called "a sneak attack on the First Amendment" by surreptitiously inserting into an appropriations bill a rider which would have compelled Rupert Murdoch to sell either the *Boston Herald*, (a paper scathingly critical of Kennedy) or his Boston T.V. station and likewise, either the *New York Post* or his New York T.V. station. Kennedy, this guardian of the Bill of Rights, would attempt to avenge his chief critic, Murdoch, by attempting to force him to sell his newspapers.

Next there was Senator Joe Biden. This paragon of morality was forced to withdraw from the presidential campaign when it was discovered that he had committed plagiarism in law school and had stolen passages from speeches of other persons, such as Robert Kennedy, Franklin D. Roosevelt, and British Labor Party leader Neil Kinnock.

Then there was Senator Patrick Leahy. An individual who would accuse Judge Bork of insensitivity to the poor because he never did *pro bono* work. In effect, Bork had done *pro bono* work all his life, since he had

for most of his career served in government and academic positions where, as a servant of the public and
as an educator of new lawyers, he had received far less
pay than he could have earned in private practice. In
fact, as he told the committee in an emotionally choked
voice after being pressed by Leahy, he only served as
a partner with a law firm in private practice after he
was forced to do so in order to pay the medical expenses
of his late wife while she was dying of cancer. Yet this
paragon of virtue, Senator Leahy, committed an action
with the substantial potential for destruction of trust
in the sharing of intelligence matters between the
Executive branch and Congress when he leaked to the
press secret documents to which he had access as
chairman of the Senate Intelligence Committee. As a
result of such action, this paragon of virtue, Patrick
Leahy, was forced to resign as Intelligence Committee
chairman.

Rounding out this stellar quartet is Howard
Metzenbaum.

For the Jewish community, Howard Metzenbaum
is a particular source of embarrassment. As Jews, we
know that any unethical transaction of any member of
the Jewish community is automatically reflected on
the community as a whole, and is exploited by anti-
Semites. We all know that the criminal actions of Ivan
Boesky, et als. on Wall Street and the Donald Maneses
and Stanley Friedmans in New York City had the
effect of disgracing the entire Jewish community.
Thus, when an individual in the public eye, like
Howard Metzenbaum, who publicly portrays himself
as an advocate of the Jewish community, then engages
in the highest degree of unethical political practice,
such lack of scruples only adds fuel to the fire of anti-
Semites.

Howard Metzenbaum began his career of political
ethical charlatanism in the 1970 Democratic primary
campaign in Ohio for United States Senator when he
accused his ultimately victorious opponent, former
astronaut and United States Marine Corps Colonel
John Glenn, of never having held a regular job. This
slur against a patriotic American, however, redounded
to his detriment when Glenn in a debate dared
Metzenbaum to tell Gold Star mothers who had lost
their children in wars that their sons had never held a
regular job. Metzenbaum's insensitivity was shocking,
and it is somewhat remarkable that he ever rebounded
to win a United States Senate seat in 1976.

Metzenbaum is very much a member of the most
leftward liberal branch of the Democratic party within
the United States Senate. The philosophy of the Reagan Administration is totally abhorrent to him, and
he began a pattern of reckless accusations of unethical
conduct against Attorney General Edwin Meese during the 1984 hearings on the confirmation of Meese as
Attorney General. During these hearings, however, it
was revealed that Senator Metzenbaum had received
$250,000 as a "finder's fee" from a long-time political
supporter and campaign contributor, Jeffrey I. Friedman, for the Senator's role in the sale of the Hay
Adams, a posh Washington hotel owned by Mr. Friedman in partnership with a French businessman. The
buyer's Washington representative was totally
unaware of the fact that Senator Metzenbaum was
receiving the finder's fee, and the transaction had all
the appearance of a kickback from a campaign contributor. In fact, the amount of money received by
Senator Metzenbaum on this transaction was over
three times his Senate salary of $72,600 per year. The

rules of the House of Representatives forbid its members from earning outside income equal to more than 30 percent of their annual salary! It is the height of hypocrisy that a man like Howard Metzenbaum, who poses as a man of high ethics appalled by the Reagan administration, should engage in a transaction that has the absolute worst appearance of impropriety.

Out of embarrassment, Senator Metzenbaum returned the finder's fee when it received news coverage during the Meese hearings. Metzenbaum shamelessly proceeded on his phony ethical crusade against Reagan administration appointees. During the Bork hearings, however, he crowned his ethical hypocrisy with a display of incompetence as well.

This display of incompetence occurred during his questioning of Bork, when he noted that Bork's actions as Solicitor General in firing Archibald Cox, the Watergate Special Prosecutor during the Nixon administration was declared illegal by a District of Columbia Federal District Court Judge. What Metzenbaum failed to note was that this ruling was ultimately overturned by the District of Columbia, United States Circuit Court of Appeals! To cite an overturned case as authority for anything is the height of legal malpractice, demonstrating gross incompetence on the part of a United States Senator.

The display of shameless ethical charlatanism by his staff was yet to come, however,

As mentioned above, Linda Greene, an aide to Metzenbaum, telephoned the aforementioned Professor John T. Baker on the eve of his scheduled testimony before the Senate Judiciary Committee, advising him to expect difficult questioning and hardball tactics. The Kerrison article mentioned above stated that she allegedly said to Baker, "our strategy will be to focus on you, to make you look silly and foolish."

This advice had the effect of intimidating Baker, and he cancelled his scheduled appearance. By not firing Greene or in any way repudiating her, Metzenbaum, in effect, condoned her actions.

Intimidating a witness before a judicial trial or a Congressional hearing is the height of ethical malfeasance. Metzenbaum's ethical record has now reached a stage of total embarrassment to the American Jewish community at large. It is all the more saddening that Metzenbaum's pattern of ethical charlatanism became most evident to the American electorate at a time when many of the Jewish community's most prominent liberal members were engaged in the defeat of perhaps the most qualified candidate for the Supreme Court during the last half century; a man who more than anyone else would have followed in the traditions of perhaps the two greatest Jewish jurists in history, Louis Brandeis and Felix Frankfurter. We can only be thankful for the Rabbi Handlers, who made sure the Senate knew that the American Jewish Congress and the Howard Metzenbaums did not speak for the American Jewish community at large.

Chapter 12
Judaism and American Liberalism

"We are now engaged in a great struggle against Nazism and Communism. In order that the Allies may be victorious, they will have to pay a tremendous price for the victory of freedom of God and of faith."
—Rabbi Herbert S. Goldstein, Professor of Homiletics, Yeshiva University and Rabbi, West Side Institutional Synagogue, New York, in his 1957 book, *Between the Lines of the Bible*

Rabbi Goldstein's book, *Between the Lines of the Bible*, is a complete commentary of each of the 613 mitzvoth (commandments) of the Torah. The Torah and its various commentaries, such as the Talmud, Midrash, and various Rabbinical tractates, elucidate not only a total philosophy of life but also a complete ritual according to which Jews are required to conduct their daily affairs.

A totalitarian regime attempts to impose an ideology governing each aspect of the daily lives of its citizens. Such a dictatorship is naturally hostile to any counter-ideology of any of its minority groups, and therefore, will be virulent in persecuting practicing Jews. This is why the three leading totalitarian regimes of the twentieth century, to wit, Nazi Germany, the Communist Soviet Union, and the Islamic fundamentalist Khomini regime in Iran have also been the three worst persecutors of Jews. By contrast, in an *authoritarian* dictatorship, such as under the Shah of Iran or Somoza's Nicaragua, in which the dictator is simply concerned with maintaining his monopoly power and wealth and not with the daily rituals of the citizens, Jews can survive and freely practice their Judaism.

Thus, in 1957, it was perfectly natural for Rabbi Goldstein to cite Nazism and Communism as enemies of the Jewish people. Thirty years later, however, the tendency of Jewish liberals is to practice an "anti-anti-Communism," claiming that Jews who put too much emphasis on combatting the Soviet Union and the spread of Communism are not being true to the traditions and practices of our people.

There are factors in Jewish history which have led Jewish liberals to often condone and rationalize the practices of certain Communist regimes, but these historical factors have nothing to do with Judaism per se. As I noted in the introduction to this book, Jewish life in the late nineteenth and early twentieth centuries in Russia, Lithuania and Poland was dominated by Czarist pogroms. Therefore, Jews often mistakenly viewed Russian Communists as liberators of Jewry from Czarist oppression. Unfortunately, history would soon reveal that Russian Jews had merely traded one set of oppressors for another. Jewish liberals later mistakenly viewed Soviet participation in World War II against the Nazis as proof positive that Jews should not be obsessed by opposition to Communism. What these Jewish liberals forgot is that initially the Soviets and Nazis began World War II as allies, sharing in the conquest of Poland.

In an article written for the *New York Post* on Tuesday, September 29, 1987 entitled "Judaism versus Liberalism," Norman Podhoretz notes another historical reason for Jewish antipathy toward the right. As he states, until recent times, the left of center Western political parties (with the exception of the Communists) were as a rule more supportive of Jewish interests than parties of the right. As Podhoretz also points out, "conversely, anti-Semitism generally used to find a more comfortable home on the right than on the left (once more with the great exception of the Communists)."

Today, however, this historical experience is but a memory. American liberals now espouse a credo totally at odds with Jewish interests, as I have describe throughout this book, in areas of foreign policy, racial quotas, and anti-Semitism from the left, such as that of Gore Vidal and Jesse Jackson (as also noted by Podhoretz). Therefore, there remains no valid historical reason for Jews to espouse liberalism and incorporate it as part and parcel of Jewish theology. To judge the compatibility of Judaism with the theology of liberalism, it is high time for both Jewish liberals and conservatives to examine the theology of Judaism itself.

*   *   *   *   *

In both Protestantism and Catholicism, liberal theologians have been active in recent years in propounding a "social agenda" to move their respective churches in a leftward direction on five basic issues: 1) birth control; 2) abortion; 3) capital punishment; 4) pacifism; and 5) homosexuality. In each of these areas the teachings of traditional Judaism are totally antithetical to the new social agenda of the liberal clergy.

The liberal clergy in each religion has attempted to reconcile birth control with its particular traditional theology. As outlined by Rabbi David M. Feldman in his landmark book, *Marital Relations, Birth Control, and Abortion in Jewish Law,* under Jewish law there are ways in which females may practice birth control. However, it is not necessarily a practice to be encouraged or mandated; in fact, the very first Mitzvah of Jewish law is found in the first chapter of Genesis, verse 28, in which G-d commands humanity to "Be fruitful and multiply." In fact, as I have mentioned previously in this book, it is in the interest of the Jewish community in both Israel and the United States to increase their respective birth rates.

On the issue of capital punishment, the liberal clergy, including liberal Jewish rabbis, have campaigned vigorously for the abolition of the death penalty, even in cases of the most heinous crimes. In the Torah, however, capital punishment is not only authorized; is is, in fact, mandated in the case of murder, as stated in Exodus, Chapter 21, verse 12.

The liberal clergy have inveighed continuously against the "evils of our military-industrial complex." They lend support to movements such as the "nuclear freeze" and unilateral disarmament. Yet Judaism is, if anything, a highly anti-pacifist creed. Our sages teach us that when we know somebody is about to murder us, we are commanded to "kill him before he kills you." In the book of Deuteronomy, while the children of Israel are required to offer peace before entering into the war, if they know that the enemy will not make peace, then the Israelites are commanded to wage total war against their adversaries (Deuteronomy, Chapter 20, verses 10–14). There is no way that Jewish pacifists can reconcile their pacifist credo with Jewish law.

In the area of homosexuality, the liberal clergy

have aligned themselves with those advocating a policy of "gay rights." Yet in Judaism, homosexuality is regarded as an obnoxious form of perversion. In Leviticus, Chapter 18, verse 22, it is written "thou shalt not lie with mankind, as with womankind: it *is* an abomination." In fact, the Torah, in Deuteronomy, Chapter 22, verse 5, goes so far as to prohibit the wearing of women's clothes by men. ("Neither shall a man put on a woman's garment; for whosoever doeth these things is an abomination unto the Lord, thy G-d.")

On the issue of abortion, the liberal Christian clergy have attempted to abrogate church dogma, particularly in Catholicism, which defines abortion as murder. As I have noted in Chapter Seven, while Judaism does not define abortion as murder, it is deemed to be a sin, to wit, the destruction of potential life, except in the case of the necessity to save the mother's life.

Thus, the Torah is clearly not consistent with the new liberal theology which has emerged in Protestantism and Catholicism and is now being propagated by a certain segment of the Jewish clergy, particularly among reform Rabbis. Furthermore, there is virtually no possibility that Orthodox Judaism will ever accept such a distortion of the Torah.

In an excellent article entitled "The Kosher Majority" appearing in the April 10, 1987 issue of the *National Review*, the highly respected conservative columnist Don Feder, himself a member of a traditional congregation in Dover, Massachusetts, outlines in depth how Orthodoxy, traditionally the least political branch of Judaism, has begun to assert itself on the same social issues that have normally been identified with the Gentile religious right. He notes that in the spring of 1986, when New York City enacted a highly controversial gay-rights ordinance, the chief opponents of the bill were the Archdiocese of New York and the leaders of the city's Orthodox Jewish community.

As Feder notes, the traditional reluctance of Orthodox Rabbis to engage in political involvement originated in the ghetto where it was considered unwise to "meddle in the affairs of gentiles." This reluctance is being abandoned. With the numerical growth of Orthodoxy, furthered by the growth of Jewish day schools and spurred by the efforts of the proselytizing Lubavitcher Chasidic movement, Orthodox Jewry is emerging as a key component of the social issues New Right coalition.

If there is any doubt about the vehemence of Orthodox rabbis on social issues, such doubts are quickly dismissed by the following statements which Feder has quoted:

On abortion, Agudath Israel, the social service organization acting as the lobbying arm of Orthodox Judaism has stated:

"Jewish law teaches that all human life is sacred. The life of a fetus has status and dignity. Agudath Israel supports legislation that protects fetal life by restricting the availability of abortion on demand."

Echoing this sentiment, the Union of Orthodox Jewish Congregations (UOJC) has promulgated the following position:

"...abortion is not a private matter between a woman and her physician...it infringes upon the most fundamental right of a third party—that of the unborn child. For Jews, fetal life is inviolate unless continuation of the pregnancy poses a serious threat to the life of the mother."

On the issue of homosexuality, Feder again quotes the Union of Orthodox Jewish Congregations, whose official position is that "the Jewish religious tradition deems homosexual relations as a serious offense, proscribed by biblical injunction." Feder further quotes the UOJC's Executive Vice President, Rabbi Pinchas Stolper, as stating that gay rights "represents an attack on the morality of a society whose laws are designed to protect and preserve family, morality, marriage and procreation."

Feder even notes in the article that there is significant support among the leadership of Orthodox Jewry for prayer in public schools, to wit, Rabbi Menachem Schneerson, the highly revered *rebbe* of the Lubavitcher Chasidim, who has stated, "If we want the next generation of children to grow up as productive moral human beings, they must be given the opportunity during school hours to meditate on matters of vital importance—their purpose in life and the belief in the Creator and Ruler of the World."

As for myself, I am a conservative Jew who does not necessarily agree with all the aforesaid Orthodox theology. I substantially concur, however, on the issue of "gay rights." It is one thing to argue that homosexuals who do not flaunt their homosexuality should be left alone to practice their own life styles in the privacy of their own homes. It is another thing to contend that homosexuality must be accepted as an equally valid life style and that open homosexuals may be hired for such sensitive positions as public school teachers and government security positions. To equate discrimination on the basis of race with discrimination on the basis of homosexuality is the height of intellectual dishonesty. Race is an immutable characteristic which is irrelevant to one's qualification for any position. Homosexuality involves aberrant behavior (and lethal as well; i.e. AIDS), which is a matter of one's voluntary choice. A homosexual may either refrain from this aberrant behavior or may at least conduct his perversion behind closed doors. Nobody forces him to flaunt his deviancy.

I have quoted all these Rabbis and religious sources not to argue that Jews are not free to dissent from the Orthodox Jewish point of view on various contemporary moral and political issues. I do feel, however, that it is essential to examine the Torah itself and the views of those who most closely adhere to it, to wit, Orthodox Jewry, in examining whether contemporary political liberalism has any real basis in traditional Judaism. To this question, the answer must be a resounding *no*.

The Torah remains as the most precious testament given by Jewry to Western civilization. While it has been reinterpreted by such scholars as Rabbis Moses Maimonides, Rashi, and Vilna Gaon, it has never been rewritten, even by these eminent sages. It remains the Torah of Moses and not the Torah of the Democratic National Committee.

Chapter 13
The Holocaust and Liberal Opportunism

"Churchill showed more interest in the Jewish situation than Roosevelt and was more compassionate, but even he was not willing to devote much thought to the subject."
—Walter Laqueur, in *The Terrible Secret*

The Holocaust is normally thought of as mankind's worst example of bestiality. For one who has faith in the ultimate decency of mankind, however, almost as horrifying as the Holocaust itself was the indifference of Western leaders to it and the continuing willingness to allow perpetrators to remain unpunished.

The responsibility for this appalling history of shameful apathy and, in fact, connivance with Nazi fugitives is definitely bipartisan. Only the most outrageously partisan Democrat or Republican could claim that his party had displayed greater concern and efforts in saving the lives of Jewish refugees and obstructing the trains transporting Jews to the extermination camps.

The Democratic Party's record has been well documented, particularly that of Franklin D. Roosevelt. As described in Chapter 8, the Roosevelt administration, while fully committed to the destruction of Nazi tyranny, per se, basically ignored the fact that Hitler was waging not only a war against the Western Allies and Soviets, but another war against the Jews and that in the latter war, as Chaim Weizmann stated, Hitler may be said to have won a great victory. The Roosevelt Administration had an outstanding record in faithfully granting Lend-Lease assistance to the British and Soviets while the Nazis were threatening their survival. No such Lend-Lease, however, existed for European Jewry. Not a single American bomb fell on the rail lines carrying European Jewry to the extermination camps. For those Jews who escaped the butcher, the doors of Roosevelt's America were closed to immigration. Meanwhile, as Walter Laqueur has written in *The Terrible Secret*, American foreign policy makers actually played down news of the Holocaust.

When one thinks of the Nazis, one usually focuses on the individuals at the top of the Nazi hierarchy who were tried in Nuremberg, to wit, the Goerings, Streichers, and those who avoided trial by suicide or escape such as Himmler, Goebbels, Bormann and Eichmann. However, in the words of my German history professor at Northwestern, James Sheehan, a few lunatics could not have created the Holocaust. Rather, it was a total effort on the part of the Nazi bureaucracy. The Eichmanns, Himmlers and Heydrichs may never have actually participated in the tortures and gassings of a single person. The prison guards, sadists, and execution squad commanders often escaped justice and succeeded in effecting the final ghoulish irony by finding a refuge from justice in the United States. They were aided by a CIA which was duped into thinking that the Klaus Barbies and their ilk were vitally needed to contain the Soviet threat. Thus, the CIA and often American immigration officials enabled former Nazis to find a haven in either the United States or South America.

All this CIA and Immigration and Naturalization Service activity actually originated in the Truman administration. I am not blaming Harry Truman, individually, but it was his administration that allowed this activity to commence.

Yet the Republican party has hardly offered a more satisfactory alternative on the issue of the Holocaust and its aftermath.

In his epic book, *Wanted: The Search for Nazis in North America*, Howard Blum writes at length about Nicolae Malaxa, the chief financial benefactor of the Iron Guard, the Nazi collaborationist army in Romania. When Malaxa attempted to immigrate to the United States after the Second World War, one of the sponsors of a private bill in Congress to admit him for immigration was the then U.S. Senator from California, Richard M. Nixon.

Furthermore, when one examines the history of America's response to Nazism, one must remember that it was the right wing of the Republican party of the 1930's that spearheaded the isolationist philosophy which inhibited Roosevelt from taking any action against the Nazis. While today, it is the left-wing Democrats in the Congress (e.g. Solarz, Gejedenson, Levine, et als.) who obstruct American action against Sandinista totalitarianism and anti-Semitism in Nicaragua, in the 1930's, it was the conservative *Republican* isolationists (e.g. Senators Borah, Nye, and Representative Hamilton Fish) who obstructed American resistance to Nazi tyranny.

Thus, there is plenty of blame to assess against both political parties. Neither party can claim a monopoly on virtue regarding issues involving the Holocaust. Furthermore, as a matter of pure elemental decency anyone but the most callous individual would refrain from attempting to woo Jewish voters with a "Holocaust Appeal." For any American Jew, particularly Holocaust survivors, the Holocaust is not an ordinary academic or even emotional concern. It is an actual live memory of parents, siblings and children being tortured or gassed, of having tattoos imposed on one's arm by SS and Gestapo monsters. To use the Holocaust as a partisan political issue to appeal for political support from people who have suffered the most extreme hells is the height of gall and insensitivity.

Yet such gall and insensitivity was found in the person of Elizabeth Holtzman, presently the District Attorney of Brooklyn and former member of the U.S. House of Representatives. In an article in the May 1, 1987 issue of the *New York Times*, entitled "Speed up the Deportation of Ex-Nazis," Holtzman accused the Reagan administration of having "ambivalence towards the Nazi legacy." Evidently, due to her own selective political morality, Ms. Holtzman chose to ignore the fact that the Reagan administration had by far the best record of any Presidency on Holocaust related issues. This is the administration that succeeded in obtaining passage of the Genocide Convention in Congress and gave unswerving support to the establishment of a Holocaust memorial. Indeed, this is the administration which barred Austrian President, Kurt Waldheim from entry into the United States because of his Nazi war record. Finally, this is the administration that prevented a *second* Holocaust by its support of the transport of the Ethiopian Jewish community to Israel.

Yet Ms. Holtzman attributed the "Reagan

administration's ambivalence toward the Nazi legacy" as one of three factors contributing to the delay of the deportation of Nazi Karl Linnas to the Soviet Union. The two other factors she mentioned were 1) "a maze of redundant legal proceedings surrounding the deportation process;" and 2) "an unconscionable government policy, lasting almost 30 years, of condoning the presence of Nazi war criminals in America." The latter factor is most interesting in view of her singling out the Reagan administration for condemnation. This "unconscionable Government policy" began in the Truman administration. It consisted, in her own words of "a secret policy of collaborating with Nazi war criminals. As part of a Cold War strategy, government agencies worked with Nazis abroad and even brought them to this country, sometimes in violation of presidential orders and sometimes by deceiving other governmental agencies. In addition, an estimated 10,000 Nazi war criminals came here on their own. The government took virtually no action against them for 29 years. Mr. Linnas was in this group."

It is interesting to note that this policy began in the administration of Harry Truman and continued through three Democratic administrations, namely John F. Kennedy, Lyndon B. Johnson, and Jimmy Carter. Yet in an outrageous—in fact ghoulish—display of hypocrisy, only the Reagan administration—which actually has the best record in bringing Nazi war criminals to justice—is singled out by Ms. Holtzman as having an "ambivalence toward the Nazi legacy." Ms. Holtzman further states that Mr. Linnas admitted to the *New York Times* in 1961 that he had been in charge of guard duty for some months at a concentration camp. Yet no investigation was conducted into his past, nor was any effort made at that time to strip him of his citizenship. The Democratic and liberal Kennedy and Johnson administrations—which did nothing about Linnas—receive no criticism from Ms. Holtzman; the Reagan administration—which actually did deport Linnas—is excoriated.

Finally, Ms. Holtzman engages in hideous distortion and slander by claiming that the Reagan administration has participated in a cover-up of the records of former Nazi war criminals at the United Nations. The fact of the matter is, however, that the Reagan administration followed the exact same policy as its Democratic predecessors regarding these files during Reagan's first term; however, it is the Reagan administration which in the second term actually *changed* this policy by working with Israel to press the Secretary General to broaden access to these files. Yet once again, Ms. Holtzman singles out the Reagan administration for criticism while its Democratic predecessors escape Ms. Holtman's self-righteous wrath.

There is a reason for her hypocrisy. Like most American Jewish liberals, she realizes that her party and her fellow liberals have begun to lose the allegiance of the American Jewish voters. Thus, such Jewish liberal politicians will attempt to retain the loyalties of Jewish voters by demagogic slanders of the Reagan administration on an issue of ultra-sensitivity to American Jews.

Ms. Holtzman has distinguished herself politically as a person of selective political morality. As pointed out by conservative lawyer, William Rusher in an August, 1987 CNN Larry King show, she was at the forefront of those seeking the impeachment of Richard M. Nixon and was also a most severe critic of the White

House and Attorney General Edwin Meese during the Iran-Contra Affair; yet she uttered hardly a word of criticism against liberal Democrat Senator Patrick Leahy of Vermont when he leaked secret documents to which he had access as chairman of the Senate Intelligence Committee. No action taken by the Reagan administration was more damaging *than that of Senator Leahy* to trust in the sharing of intelligence between the President and Congress; however, Ms. Holtzman invoked her selective morality and has spared Senator Leahy her wrath.

There are two urgent priorities on the American Jewish agenda regarding the Holocaust. The first is to educate our fellow citizens as to what actually happened during that dark era of our history to ensure that no people will ever again be subject to genocide. The second is the establishment of a bipartisan consensus for bringing Nazis to justice. This objective, however, is hardly furthered by selective moralists like Ms. Holtzman making the issue a political football.

Perhaps Ms. Holtzman's selective morality is not uncommon among ambitious politicians, but when liberal Jews play politics with the Holocaust, it is more than politics as usual—it is an obscenity.

And as this book went to press, Elizabeth Holtzman was still under fire for statements she made in 1987 accusing a Brooklyn judge of forcing a rape victim to re-enact the crime. These accusations were later determined to be false by a state investigator. At the very least, Ms. Holtzman was guilty of gross negligence in making her accusations. It is highly unethical for a prosecutor to play fast and loose with the truth, as she did in this case. Yet any informed reader who read her aforementioned *Times* article should not have been surprised at her propensity to do so.

Ms. Holtzman made a career of accusing others of unethical conduct as a member of the U.S. House of Representatives. It will be interesting to see how she reacts now that the ethical mirror is turned on her.

Chapter 14
The Jews and South Africa

"The Western democracies, whose basic values are freedom and human rights, should continue to protest long and loud, against all the miserable practices of Apartheid and to use all positive measures to speed its demise. But moral indignation should not lead them to impose punitive measures that will wreck the economy of the country in which black South Africans will inevitably share."
—Helen Suzman, in the *New York Times*, October 4, 1987

The racially oppressive system of Apartheid existing in South Africa is repugnant to the very core of Jewish values. Jews of all political persuasions can unite in their advocacy of an end to Apartheid in South Africa and the establishment in that nation of a system of universal suffrage, civil liberties and equal rights for all races, colors, and creeds.

Unfortunately, this lofty goal is often obfuscated by the insistence of American liberals that economic sanctions be imposed against South Africa. Furthermore, American liberals blindly support the ascension to power of the Marxist oriented African National Congress and its leading ally in the clergy, to wit, Nobel prize-winner, Bishop Desmond Tutu.

For any thoughtful American Jew, both these canons of American liberal dogma are at best foolhardy and counter-productive and at worst a prescription for the devastation of the Jewish community in South Africa. American Jewish liberals have totally ignored the anti-Zionist dogma of the African National

Congress and the outright anti-Semitic pronouncements of Bishop Tutu, more of which will be discussed
later in this chapter. Since it is the hope of the American Left that sanctions will result in the ascension to
power of the African National Congress and its allies,
it is appropriate that we first examine the issue of
economic sanctions and their likely effect.

*   *   *   *   *

Throughout history, economic growth in a society
has been the greatest engine for upward mobility of
oppressed classes. No one should understand this
better than the American Jew. The early twentieth-
century American Jewish community was in large
part composed of recent immigrants from Eastern
Europe. These impoverished new arrivals were subjected to a significant degree of anti-Semitism mani-
festing itself in discrimination in employment, housing, and admittance to educational institutions. It was
the expansion of the American economy throughout
the twentieth century that subsequently enabled Jews
to achieve their greatest prosperity in the history of
Western civilization. Likewise, the expansion of the
South African economy, supported by Western capital
investment, has resulted in the improvement of the
economic lot of the black South African to such an
extent that blacks from neighboring black-dominated
countries have streamed into South Africa to seek
employment opportunity.

Let me emphasize that I am making no apology for
Apartheid. Despite the improvement in the economic
lot of the black South African, racism and discrimination continue to inflict an appalling misery on their

lives. If there is to be any hope for the peaceful destruction of Apartheid, however, America should actually *expand* its economic investment in South Africa, while simultaneously requiring American companies operating plants there to abide by the "Sullivan Principles" of non-discrimination in the employment of workers and managers for these facilities.

An October 12, 1987 *Wall Street Journal* editorial entitled "Beyond Sanctions" documented the direct relationship between the growth of South African black economic power and the erosion of Apartheid. This editorial supported the assertion of former Assistant U.S. Secretary of State, Alan Keyes that blacks have achieved their most significant victories over Apartheid in the economy. The editorial pointed out that since the legalization of black trade unions in 1979, their membership has increased from 120,000 to 1,000,000. Furthermore, since the legalization of black ownership and operation of transit systems in 1984, there are now approximately 40,000 black-owned cabs in South Africa. Even more remarkably, a black group is now seeking majority ownership of Putco, described by the editorial as "the largest private transit company in the South Hemisphere." As further stated in the editorial, "the erosion of economic Apartheid through civil disobedience and lax enforcement has created over 100,000 small black businesses in the past decade."

It should clearly be the policy of Western democracies to promote the destruction of Apartheid by *increased* investment in South Africa with the intended goal of promoting the expansion of black economic power. Instead, Western economic sanctions have produced the exact opposite effect. The

aforementioned *Wall Street Journal* editorial noted
that the endangerment of the overseas market for the
South African fruit industry (due to sanctions) had
resulted in the lay-off of some 40,000 of its 220,000
non-white workers. Furthermore, the editorial noted
that the militant black trade union group, COSATU
has warned that increased disinvestment and sanctions could result in the unemployment of an additional two million blacks by the year 2000. Anyone who
is truly concerned about the welfare of South African
blacks must therefore deplore Western sanctions.
Their counter-productivity has been a continuing
expressed concern of Helen Suzman, a South African
Jewess, who is the longest serving member of Parlia-
ment in South Africa and the spokesperson for the
Progressive Federal Party, the leading anti-Apartheid
white political party. Ms. Suzman, at personal risk to
herself, opposed Apartheid before it was fashionable.
As she stated in the *New York Times* article quoted in
the beginning of this chapter, "The sad truth of the
matter is that there is no instant solution that will
transform the South African scene...*The most effective
instrument for change is economic expansion within
the country. This is the force that led in the first
instance to those non-cosmetic changes that have taken
place in the last ten years—the opening of skilled jobs
to blacks, improvements in education and training,
recognition of black trade unions, acceptance of a
permanent black urban population and the abolition of
the pass laws.*"

Yet as Ms. Suzman notes in the article, "the
absence of foreign investment capital and the withdrawal of foreign companies (especially American
firms fed up with the hassle factor and the threat of

boycotts at home) have reduced the growth rate to less than the minimum required to keep job opportunities level with new job seekers." Thus, while American liberals take great moral self-satisfaction by the passage of sanctions legislation, their newly-enacted measures are undoing all the progress made by South African blacks in the economic and political spheres during the past decade.

Yet many American liberals, while conceding the short-term deleterious effect sanctions have had on the economic and political status of South African blacks, continue to espouse sanctions in the hope that they would result in a weakening of the existing white ruling parties. However, as Ms. Suzman states in the *Times* article, sanctions have had precisely the reverse effect. As she notes, the election last May for South Africa's white assembly resulted in a distinct shift to the right. The key factors prompting this shift were: 1) a campaign appealing to security fears of the white minority; 2) appeals against "outside interference." President P.W. Botha's National Party received 123 seats out of 166. Yet even more damaging to the opponents of Apartheid was the success of the ultra-right wing Conservative party. This party captured 22 seats and displaced the Progressive Federal Party as the official opposition. Following the election, Botha reimposed the state of emergency and tightened press censorship.

Thus, the political and economic case against sanctions is abundantly compelling. Unfortunately, Israel, under pressure from American Congressional liberals, joined in this madness on September 16, 1987 by announcing various sanctions against South Africa, including the freezing of all steel imports from South

Africa, the cessation of trade of oil products with South Africa and the banning of use of Israeli ports as transit stations for shipping of goods to or from South Africa.

Yet it must be said that at least the Israelis realize the dangers of the ascension to power by anti-Western black community elements. Such political movements have as their heart and core an anti-Zionist and in fact, anti-Semitic philosophy that many American Jewish liberals conveniently ignore.

Both conservative and liberal Americans agree that universal suffrage is fair, appropriate, just, and long overdue in South Africa. Yet any rational Western thinker must be concerned that the transition to black majority rule does not result in: 1) the persecution of the white community, many of whose members had nothing to do with the maintenance of the system of Apartheid; and 2) the ascension to power of a communist regime, which by its very nature would be anti-democratic and hostile to all ethnic minorities viewed as Western-oriented, including the Jewish community.

There are many black South Africans who are both anti-Apartheid and anti-communist, most notably, Chief Buthelezi, the leader of the Zulu tribe, who in no way can be viewed as a Black African Uncle Tom. Most American leading liberals, however, discount Chief Buthelezi and instead regard as the authentic voice of Black South Africa Nobel prize winner, Bishop Desmond Tutu.

In the summer of 1985, Jerry Falwell visited South Africa and returned to the United States voicing opposition to economic sanctions. Among other things, he labeled Bishop Tutu as a "phony." For this comment, Falwell was excoriated by leading American liberals, including many leaders of the American Jewish community.

Perhaps these Jewish liberals would have been less eager to lambast Falwell and come to Tutu's defense if they had known of various statements Tutu had made regarding Jews and Israel. A record of these statements was published in the *Jewish Press* on Friday, March 13, 1987. This issue reported that Tutu had, in a 1984 speech in New York, accused Jews of displaying "an arrogance—the arrogance of power because Jews are a powerful lobby in this land." The *Jewish Press* also reported that Tutu had spoken to Jewish leaders in South Africa and charged that Jews are "the biggest exploiters of blacks in South Africa" and threatened that "there will be no sympathy for the Jews when the Blacks take over." Further the *Jewish Press* reported various statements of Eliahu Lankin, the former Israeli Ambassador to South Africa, to the Israel News Bulletin regarding meetings he had held with Bishop Tutu while Lankin was stationed in Pretoria. According to Lankin, "Tutu refused to call Israel by its name, he kept referring to it as 'Palestine'." Lankin also recalled that Tutu "used standard PLO arguments and rhetoric while accusing Israel of 'oppressing the Palestinians.'"

Lankin acknowledged that "Jews cannot easily swallow the idea of racial discrimination." He warned, however, that "if Tutu and (Nelson) Mandela (the founder and hero of the African National Congress) take over, it could lead to total physical extermination of all white in South Africa, including the 110,000 Jews there."

In spite of Lankin's warnings about Tutu, Mandela, and the African National Congress, and in spite of Helen Suzman's statements about the counter-productivity of sanctions, American Jewish liberals continue to be at the forefront of the movement advocating economic sanctions and supporting the ascension to power of Mandela and Tutu. Certainly, American Jewish liberal leaders are free to express their opinions on South Africa; however, they cannot legitimately lend the official imprimatur of the American Jewish community to this movement and claim that it is in the interest of South African Jewry as well.

South Africa has a thriving Jewish community which comprises six percent of the population. According to an article written by Geoffrey Fisher in 1976 in the *San Francisco Bulletin*, Jews account for a quarter of South Africa's total output. This community, which had its origins in the 17th century, has also produced a thriving Jewish culture. According to an article written by Arnold Fine in the *Jewish Press* on Friday, November 27, 1987, approximately 33 percent of the entire Jewish school-going population in South Africa attend Jewish day schools. In fact, according to Fine, South Africa has the highest percentage in the world of any Jewish community regarding the number of Jewish school children obtaining a Jewish education. There are four Jewish newspapers, and a number of kosher food facilities. Yet all this may soon be part of another Jewish tragedy.

The twentieth century, while witnessing the birth of the State of Israel, has been a century of disaster for Jewish communities throughout the world. First came Hitler's holocaust in the 1940's. Next came the persecution of Soviet Jewry since the 1950's. Since 1949, we have witnessed the persecution of Jews in Arab lands. Next, American Jewish liberals called for an end to the regime of the Shah of Iran. Khomeni came to power, and the first victim was the Iranian Jewish community. Now, if American Jewish liberals have their way, Tutu, Mandela and their followers will come to power in South Africa, and the first victims will be the South African Jewish community. With friends like the American Jewish liberal community, South African Jews hardly need any enemies.

Chapter 15
The Iran-Contra Affair: The Israelis and the Liberals

"It is clear, however, that Israel had its own interests, some in direct conflict with those of the United States, in having the United States pursue the initiative. For this reason, it had an incentive to keep the initiative alive...Even if the Government of Israel actively worked to begin the initiative and to keep it going, the U.S. Government is responsible for its own decisions...Although Israel dealt with those portions of the U.S. Government that it deemed were sympathetic to the initiative, there is nothing improper *per se* about this fact. U.S. decision makers made their own decisions and must bear responsibility for the consequences."
—The Tower Commission Report

I will never forget my initial reaction to the stories that began to appear in the television and print media in late 1986 regarding American arms shipments to Iran: Israel just somehow had to be involved in the transactions.

When reports then immediately emerged regarding Israel's role, I was hardly surprised. I had been reading numerous articles both by Israelis and Israel supporters since 1980 advocating that Israel and the United States tilt towards Iran in the Iran-Iraqi conflict on the basis that: 1) Khomeini was not going to live forever; and 2) Iraq, as an ally of the Soviet Union, presented a much more long-range and dangerous menace to Israel's security and American interests in the Middle East.

Any well-informed reader of articles and books on the contemporary Middle East conflict knew that it was hardly a secret that Israel was tilting towards Iran. One could question the wisdom of such a policy; however, one could not doubt that it was based upon Israel's honest appraisal of its long-term security needs. Given this motivation, it was hardly dishonorable for Israel to engage in weapon sales to Iran.

It was altogether proper once the story of arms to Iran became public for Senators and Representatives to debate the wisdom of such transactions, particularly in the context of arms for hostages. The fact of the matter is, however, that Congressional liberals were never interested in an investigation and debate into the advisability of such a foreign policy tilt. Instead, they were interested in using the transactions as a tool to destroy a very popular President, particularly after the news broke that profits from the arms sales were being diverted to the Contras in Nicaragua.

For these liberals, however, Israel's involvement in the arms sales presented an embarrassing problem. It was difficult to slash the Reagan administration for aiding Iran without attacking Israel in the process. This could result in a backlash against the liberals among Jewish voters. Therefore, liberal members of Congress initially attempted to exculpate Israel by stating that Israel had either been an unwilling partner obligated to cooperate with America due to Israeli dependence on American military assistance, or in the alternative, had been duped by Americans as to the nature of these transactions.

The evidence soon revealed, however, that far from an unwilling partner, Israel: 1) originated the idea of arms for hostages; and 2) at the very least knew about the diversion of funds to the Contras and, in fact, may have actively participated in it as well. Israel certainly had nothing to be ashamed of regarding sales to Iran since it viewed such sales as being in its national security interest; furthermore, Israel could not have been faulted if it did participate in the diversion of funds to the Contras, given the long-term alliance between the Sandinistas and the PLO.

Given these facts as a background, Israel normally would have been fully cooperative in giving testimony to Congress regarding its role in the affair. Such evidence, however, would not have served the ends of both Jewish and non-Jewish liberals in the Congress. They were determined to create a Watergate out of what was at worst a wise foreign policy executed in a horribly bungled manner. Any revelations regarding Israel's role would have impeded the liberals in their goal of "getting the President" since: 1) Israel's involvement may have actually resulted in increased support for the actions taken by the Reagan administration; and 2) the more prominently Israel's role appeared, the more likely liberal attacks against the President's policy would have resulted in a backlash against the liberals in the Jewish community.

Therefore, in order to downplay the Israeli involvement, liberal members of Congress participated in a cover-up of their own: They decided not to take the testimony of such witnesses as 1) Michael Ledeen, a former consultant for the National Security Council, who played a key role in the development of the policy and who also had close ties to senior Israeli officials, and 2) Israeli official David Kimche, who, according to Michael Ledeen, very much wanted to testify, but the Israelis refused to let him.

There is no doubt in my mind that the Israeli government would normally have had no reluctance to reveal its role in the affair. Israel knew, however, that liberals may eventually regain the White House and that therefore it could not afford to antagonize liberal Democratic members of Congress. Therefore, Israel played along with the liberal cover-up of its role in the affair. The ultimate result was: 1) a cover-up of activities that Israel had nothing to be ashamed of and consequently, 2) long-term damage to Israel's credibility.

In order to understand this, it is necessary to examine separately in depth each of my theses.

1. Israel and the Iran-Iraq War

Foreign policy is often a very unpleasant endeavor involving the survival of the fittest in the *real* world, as opposed to the *reel* world of liberalism. In conflicts involving two totalitarian powers, America must often choose between the lesser of two evil alternatives. This accounts for the American alliance with the villainous Joseph Stalin of the Soviet Union during World War II in order to fight the greater Nazi menace.

America and Israel face a similar dilemma in the Iran-Iraq War. Iran is a totalitarian state led by the maniacal Ayatollah Khomeini. Aside from traditional border disputes, his war with Iraq resulted from his desire to spread Shiite totalitarianism throughout the Fertile Crescent.

Iraq presents a different and more long-range type of menace. This nation is one of the Soviet Union's closest allies in the Middle East. It has at times approached the capability of development of nuclear weapons. This accounts for Israel's bombing of Iraq's nuclear reactor in 1981.

Early in the Iran-Iraq conflict, Israel determined that while a victory of neither Iraq nor Iran was desirable, an Iranian victory presented far fewer long-range threats to the survival and security of the State of Israel. Israel understood that a post-Khomeini Iran would probably be anti-Soviet and would contain moderate elements who might well have an opportunity to ascend to power. An Iraqi victory over Iran, however, would give the Soviets greatly enhanced power in the Middle East. Accordingly, as documented in a *Newsweek* special report, dated December 8, 1986, Israel began to sell spare parts for Iran's American-built F-4 Phantom jets as early as October, 1980. Israeli sales to Iran of spare parts, overhauled jet engines, ammunition, and other hardware reached levels of $100 million in 1983 alone.

It should be noted that leading figures in the Israeli intelligentsia also advocated a tilt to Iran. One such individual is Amos Perlmutter, an Israeli Professor of Political Science and Sociology at American University. As early as February 2, 1981, in an interview in *U.S. News and World Report*, Perlmutter advocated American moves toward immediate cooperation with Iran. In the interview, Perlmutter did oppose sales to the existing Iranian regime, unless "it warms to the U.S." Perlmutter, however, noted that "There are forces with which we can cooperate. There are pragmatists and realists among the civilian and military. Not all Ayatollahs are united in the same policies. Many are adamantly opposed to Khomeini. There are opposition elements in the middle class and in intellectual and student circles." In an article appearing in the

Wall Street Journal on Thursday, October 13, 1983, Perlmutter again noted that "There's no reason the U.S. cannot approach Iran as does Israel, which has no more implacable foe than Khomeini, yet rationally pursues a policy of clandestine neutrality, waiting for his successors." Obviously, Perlmutter was not at any point advocating Israeli arms shipments to Iran; nevertheless, it was clear that he was echoing a policy of angling towards Iran vis-a-vis Iraq. In the *Wall Street Journal* article, Perlmutter also noted that Iran had a population of 40 million, more than all the Gulf States combined. In his earlier *U.S. News and World Report* interview, he pointed out that an Iraqi victory would enable the Soviet Union to play a major role in Iranian affairs. And Iran, if nothing else, as Perlmutter pointed out in his *Wall Street Journal* article, had always maintained an anti-Soviet posture, even during the Khomeini era.

Given this known mindset of the Israeli political elite and intelligentsia, one should hardly have been surprised that Israel was engaged in clandestine arm sales to Iran.

Prior to 1985, the United States maintained a policy of neutrality in the Iran-Iraq War, although this policy was on occasion subject to pressures from the "moderate" Arab states to tilt towards Iraq. In 1985, however, prompted by the hostage crisis, the Reagan administration took a new look at its policy towards Iran.

As noted by the Tower Commission Report, the administration had a deep concern about the hostages in Beirut, Lebanon, particularly for William Buckley, the CIA Station Chief in Beirut, who was seized on March 16, 1984. According to the *Tower Commission*

Report, "Available intelligence suggested that most, if not all, of the Americans were held hostage by members of Hezballah, a fundamentalist Shiite terrorist group with links to the regime of the Ayatollah Khomeini." This interest in the hostages, combined with America's growing concern about the government in a post-Khomeini Iran, led America to seek new contacts with moderates in the Iranian Government.

At long last, American and Israeli perceptions regarding the Iran-Iraq conflict began to converge.

In 1965, Israeli officials suggested to various administration officials the notion of arm sales to Iran as a means of cementing ties with moderates in the Iranian government and thereby soliciting Iran to use its leverage with Hezballah to procure a release of the hostages. Israel volunteered itself as a conduit for the shipment of the arms. Citizens of all political orientations will long debate the wisdom of this policy, particularly the placing of the shipment of arms in the context of a deal for hostages. Certainly, however, this policy was based upon a sober evaluation of American and Israeli security interests and a humane concern for the hostages. Neither Israel nor America had anything to be ashamed of regarding the goals and outline of the policy. In essence, the subsequent liberal cover-up of Israel's role constituted a cover-up of activities of which Israel had nothing to be ashamed.

2. The Story Breaks: The Initial Liberal Reaction.

In order to understand the motivation for liberal Congressional reaction once the story of the arms shipments became public in November, 1986, one must recall the American political culture of that year.

Never during the second year of the second term of a Presidential administration had there been a more popular president than Ronald Reagan. True, his popularity was not sufficient to thwart the recapture of the U.S. Senate by the Democrats in the 1986 election. Two points, however, should be noted about this Democratic victory: 1) almost all of these victories involved races where the issues were basically local in scope; and 2) it is almost without exception the pattern for the party not controlling the White House to make significant Congressional gains in the off-year election. When one notes that the Democrats only registered a gain of four seats in the House of Representatives, their 1986 Congressional gain is actually somewhat less than normal by historical standards.

In any event, President Reagan was a towering, dominant figure on the American political landscape of 1986. His popularity enabled him to obtain the passage of such legislation as aid to the Nicaraguan freedom fighters and the 1986 Tax Reform Act. Various cover stories in news magazines trumpeted his popularity among the American public, attributing to him the greatest resurgence in the American national spirit since the administration of John F. Kennedy.

Reagan was on his way to a permanent recasting of the framework of the debate between liberals and conservatives. During the 1960's and early 1970's, the Democrats would lead off the debate by promising grandiose new spending programs to solve every sort of societal ill imaginable, and establishment conservatives would only respond by allowing as to how they too would have a program but at less cost.

Enter Ronald Reagan and the 1980's. To Reagan-

ites, the motto was "Government is the problem and
not the solution." They perceived that the vast majority of Middle America no longer believed that government could solve every problem by some expenditure
of the public purse but that, in fact, government
involvement through regulation and expenditure
could make a bad situation worse. In the area of foreign
policy, America's blunders in Viet Nam had given the
Conservative philosophy of peace through strength
and resistance to totalitarianism, be it Communism,
Nazism, or otherwise, a bad name. In the late 1970's,
however, as the world watched the Soviet Union
commit genocide in Afghanistan while President
Carter expressed "surprise," the American public
repudiated appeasement once and for all by giving
Ronald Reagan an electoral victory in 44 states. In
1984, he was the victor in all but Minnesota, the home
state of his opponent, Walter Mondale, and the
District of Columbia.

The American public had overwhelmingly opted
for Reagan's professed policies of a scaling down of
government in the domestic arena and resistance to
Soviet aggression in foreign affairs. To be sure,
Reagan's performance often fell short of his rhetoric.
Nevertheless, his *goals* were now accepted by the
American public as a permanent long-range policy,
with liberalism inexorably discredited by the American electorate.

By 1986, liberalism was faced with its most severe
crisis. The only comfort to liberals was the fact that
they had faced such a crisis earlier in the aftermath of
the 1972 Presidential election when Richard Nixon
had defeated George McGovern in every state of the
Union except Massachusetts. At that time, however,

the Watergate scandal intervened, and liberalism was given a reprieve. The liberals in Reagan's America, however, despaired that they would not be rescued by a second Watergate. True, there had been scandals and various indictments at lower levels of the Reagan administration; however, none of these cases had ever personally involved the President or damaged his credibility in any way. In fact, his critics bemusedly referred to him as a "teflon President" to whom no scandal would stick.

Thus, in late November, 1986, when the stories of the arms shipments and the diversion of funds to the Nicaraguan freedom fighters were revealed to the American public, liberal politicians rejoiced, as if they had received manna from heaven. Here was the Watergate they had been praying for, and they would proceed with all deliberate speed to use it as a sword with which to destroy their most potent adversary in contemporary American politics. The immediate liberal reaction was swift and predictable. Representative Stephen Solarz emerged from a secret meeting of the House Foreign Affairs Committee and stated that after hearing testimony, he had no doubt that the President had been totally aware of the diversion of funds to the Contras, despite the fact that others present at this Committee meeting stated that they had not heard any such evidence. Obviously, Solarz was so eager to use the story as a partisan tool with which to destroy the President that he was unwilling to wait for the presentation of all the evidence, which ultimately, in both the Tower Commission Report and the Joint Congressional hearings exonerated the President from having any such knowledge. In the case of Mr. Solarz, however, his partisanship had

totally overcome his scruples. As the attorney, Joseph
Welch said to Senator Joseph McCarthy at the height
of the Army-McCarthy hearings in 1954, one could
only say to Representative Solarz, "Have you no
shame, sir, have you no shame?"

In their haste to destroy a Presidency, however,
there was one touchy problem facing the liberal
members of Congress, particularly those with large
Jewish constituencies: the involvement of Israel. The
more prominent Israel's role appeared to be in the
transaction, the more difficult it would be for liberals
to destroy their presidential target, for two reasons:
1) Israel's involvement and the admiration as a nation
it possesses among many segments of the American
public might actually result in increased support for
the President's policies in these matters; 2) criticism of
these policies per se might be construed as criticism of
Israel, thus creating a backlash among Jewish voters
against liberal critics.

Thus, the initial task for the liberals was to find a
way to attack the President on his Iranian policy
without appearing to attack Israel in the process. The
initial liberal approach was the assertion that America had been solely responsible for the formulation and
execution of the sale of arms to Iran, with Israel being
misled into acting as a conduit. On three separate
editions of the Cable News Network Show *Crossfire*,
liberal Representatives Robert Torricelli (D-NJ, who
represents one of the largest Jewish constituencies in
the country), Sam Gejdenson, and Stephen Solarz
each asserted this argument. In the words of Representative Gejdenson, Israel was a "mouse" being led by
the American "giant."

There were basically two problems with these

arguments: 1) They were patently untrue, as would soon be displayed by new revelations about Israel's involvement; and 2) they were actually demeaning to Israel.

Had Representatives Torricelli, Gejdenson, and Solarz, been truly well informed about the Middle East, they would have read over the previous few years a spate of articles in the media by various Israelis, including the Perlmutter articles mentioned above, describing Israel's tilt towards Iran in the Iran-Iraq war. No informed reader could have in good conscience made such an argument claiming non-involvement on the part of Israel. Either Representatives Torricelli, Solarz, or Gejdenson were ill-informed, or else they were willing to play fast and easy with the truth in the interest of a partisan effort to destroy a Presidency.

Furthermore, nothing could have been more demeaning to Israel than Representative Gejdenson's analogy of Israel as "a mouse leading a giant." By implying that Israel is incapable of acting independently from American direction, Representative Gejdenson was echoing the standard Arab argument that Israel is simply "America's puppet in the Middle East." Israel is far more potent than Representative Gejdenson's mouse; in fact, it is in many ways an equal partner of the United States in an alliance that serves the interest of both parties. Its involvement with the United States in the Iranian arms shipments was likewise meant to serve the interests of both parties: 1) the Israeli interest of preventing an Iraqi victory; and 2) the American *and* Israeli interest of forging a relationship with parties who may ascend to power in a post-Khomeini Iran.

As former Defense Secretary Harold Brown noted

during his incumbency, the presence of Israel's outstanding navy in the Eastern Mediterranean enables
the United States to devote more naval resources
elsewhere. This, Mr. Gejdenson, is not a "giant-mouse"
relationship; it is a partnership of allies with mutual
respect.

In any event, as any informed reader of Middle
East politics could have predicted, new revelations
regarding Israel's involvement soon proved the falsity
of the assertions of Representatives Torricelli, Solarz,
and Gejdenson. In a subsequent edition of *Crossfire*,
Representative Solarz admitted that the idea of the
arms shipments originated in Jerusalem. He stated
that this in no way excused America's role in the
venture.

For once, Representative Solarz made a statement
I agree with. Both Israel and the United States involved themselves in the Iran-Contra policy of their
own free will.

What Representative Solarz did not say is that
while the policy may have been mistaken, it was well
motivated on the part of both the United States and
Israel. Unlike Watergate, where the involved parties
acted strictly out of partisan political motives, the
American and Israeli officials all acted out of a desire
to advance the foreign policy objectives of their respective countries. While the policy was very clumsily
executed, it certainly was well motivated by legitimate
foreign policy goals.

Yet in their haste to create a Watergate out of a
poorly executed foreign policy, the liberals, due to the
political factors mentioned above, would go to great
lengths to downplay Israel's involvement. As I will
discuss later in this Chapter, this could only work to
the long-term detriment of Israel.

3. The Contra Diversion: The Fumbles Are Multiplied

The spear with which liberal Democrats attempted to impale President Reagan was the Boland Amendments. These five amendments, enacted and effected for a time period commencing December 21, 1982 and terminating October 17, 1986, precluded the Defense Department or Central Intelligence Agency, or "any other agency or entity of the United States involved in intelligence activities" from rendering any assistance to the Contras. In addition the United States government was precluded from entering "into any arrangement conditioning, expressly or impliably, the provision of assistance by a recipient to persons or groups engaging in an insurgency or other act of rebellion" in Nicaragua. This latter provision is cited by those who claim that the diversion of the Iranian arms sale proceeds to the Contras was a violation of the Boland Amendments. (It should be noted that this prohibition against solicitation of third countries was expressly repealed by the Boland Amendment of December 4, 1985; All Boland Amendments expired as of October 17, 1986, with the Contras earlier in the year receiving authorization by the Congress of $100 million in aid.)

To this day, no two lawyers can agree on whether the diversion to the Contras constituted a violation of the Boland Amendments. It is over one year since Lawrence Walsh was appointed as Special Prosecutor, and indictments only recently have been brought against any parties. This delay indicates that it is far from clear as to whether there was any violation of the letter of the Boland Amendments. There also remains the issue as to the very constitutionality of the entire

Boland legislation, particularly whether these acts constitute an infringement of the President's authority to formulate foreign policy.

It is also important to note that if there *was* a violation of the Boland Amendments, there is ample precedent to legitimize Presidential defiance of such statutes. Indeed, prior to World War II, the then President Franklin Delano Roosevelt directly violated the Neutrality Act by trading destroyers for bases with the British and by his pre-war tracking of Nazi submarines. I doubt very much whether today's liberals would have complained about this blatant violation of the letter of the law, and neither would I. As suggested by Charles Wiley of Accuracy in Media (AIM), I also doubt whether contemporary liberals would have complained if the sales proceeds from the arms shipments to Iran had been diverted to the African National Congress.

This does not excuse in any way, however, the bumbling way in which the Reagan administration handled the diversion issue. I have long been a believer in the notion that covert operations should be confined to those activities in which secrecy is absolutely essential. I do not believe that it was necessary to conceal from the American public either the arms shipments to Iran or the diversion of funds to the freedom fighters in Nicaragua.

This was amply demonstrated by the testimony of Lieutenant Colonel Oliver North before the Joint Congressional Investigating Committee. He was very straightforward in asserting the case for both the arms shipment to Iran and the diversion to the Contras, and he received unanticipated acclaim from the American public. Had President Reagan openly challenged the legitimacy of the Boland Amendments from the outset, I have little doubt that he likewise would have received overwhelming support from the American electorate and the entire scandal would have been averted.

The real lesson from this is that the most severe damage results when you conceal from the public activities for which you have no need to maintain secrecy. Unfortunately, liberals did not learn this lesson from President Reagan's blunders, and they proceeded, for political reasons, to cover-up Israel's role in the Iran-Contra affair, when no such cover-up was needed. This cover-up, which we now examine, may result in substantial long-range damage to the credibility of Israel.

4. The Congressional Cover-Up.

As I mentioned above, liberal members of Congress had two basic motives for downplaying Israel's role in the Iran-Contra affair: 1) the possibility of a backlash in the Jewish community against liberals if they appeared to be attacking Israel; and 2) the possibility that exposure of Israel's role might result in increased public sympathy for the policy, particularly among the Jewish community.

Thus, it should have come as little surprise that liberal members of Congress proceeded with a cover-up of their own in avoiding investigation of Israel's role in the affair.

This cover-up took numerous forms. Perhaps the most blatant example of the cover-up was the Investigating Committee's failure to subpoena for public testimony Michael Ledeen, a former consultant for the National Security Council, who, in addition to formulating the policy, acted as the initial liaison with Israel and, as mentioned earlier in this Chapter, maintained close ties with many high ranking Israeli officials. Mr. Ledeen was questioned privately by Congressional investigators and was eager to testify publicly. In fact, in an article in the *Wall Street Journal* on Monday, August 3, 1987 written by Andy Pasztor and Edward T. Pound, Ledeen stated "I am the only person (from the U.S. side) who can provide first-hand testimony about the origins of this initiative."

If the Joint Congressional Investigating Committee really was interested in exploring the larger foreign policy questions of the initiative rather than simply attempting to "get Reagan," Ledeen would have been perhaps the most crucial witness in the entire hearing. Mr. Ledeen, however, doubtless would have also focussed on Israel's role in the initiative, which would not have advanced the political fortunes of the liberal members of Congress.

The cover-up, however, manifested itself in its most blatant form by the failure of the committee to question certain Israeli officials involved in the transaction, including such individuals as Amram Nir and David Kimche, two former Israeli officials, and Al Schwimmer and Yaacov Nimrodi, the Israeli arms dealers. Israel officially refused to let these individuals testify but instead, with the permission of the committee, provided a secret chronology which was never subjected to detailed examination because it arrived well after the hearings had ended.

One must question why Israel refused to cooperate with the committee. Certainly, this non-cooperation had the blessing of liberal members of Congress on the committee, including its chairman, Senator Daniel

Inouye (D-Hawaii), who in the Pasztor-Pound article in the *Wall Street Journal* praised Israel as having provided information "far beyond our expectation."

Israel's non-cooperation appears even more mysterious in view of the fact that according to Michael Ledeen, as quoted in the Pasztor-Pound article, David Kimche "badly wants to testify, but the Israeli Government won't let him." Israel in virtually every other matter of public concern involving the Middle East has always been more than cooperative with both the executive and legislative branches of our federal government.

I can only infer that Israel's policy of non-cooperation with the committee was deliberately calculated not to offend liberal members of Congress. Israel knows full well that a liberal Democratic administration may well follow the Reagan years, and it is in Israel's interest to have good relationships with liberal members of Congress who may some day be sitting in the Oval Office. The Israeli Government knew full well that if the testimony of Israeli officials was publicized, it would have appeared to be strengthening the Reagan Administration's case for the initiative. There is little benefit for the Israeli Government in supporting the incumbent administration in its "lame duck" stages.

This non-cooperation on the part of Israel, however, may cost it dearly in the long run in terms of support from the American people. Israel is perhaps America's major ally in terms of military and economic assistance. If the public perceives Israel as having a major impact on American foreign policy without a willingness to have any accountability for it, then such continuing military and economic assistance may well be endangered. This is particularly true if Israel, in addition to being viewed as not accountable for its actions, is also viewed as being less than candid.

There are already signs that this withholding of evidence on the part of Israel may have affected Israel's standing in the Congress among conservative members who would normally be expected to support the Jewish State. The Pasztor-Pound article described above quoted Representative Henry Hyde (R-Illinois) as stating "the role played by Israel in initiating and then sustaining the initiative with Iran has been virtually ignored." According to the article, both Representative Hyde and Senator James McClure (R-Idaho) contend that a closer examination of Israel's role is crucial to understanding the origins of American involvement.

As Senator McClure points out, the damage to Israel from exposure of the affair was far less than that incurred by America. Therefore, one must wonder why Israel has been so reluctant to cooperate. The most probably answer lies in the reluctance of Israeli officials to alienate liberal members of Congress who, as mentioned before, have every political motive to conceal Israel's involvement.

Regardless of what motivated Israeli officials to conceal the nature and extent of Israel's role, many American Jews express relief that Congress has not subjected Israel's role to closer scrutiny. These individuals fear that any further revelations about Israel's activities could well endanger the "clean and moral" image Israel now has among the vast majority of the American electorate.

I dissent completely, however, from the notion that American public opinion would in any way be tilted against Israel as a result of further revelations. The American electorate understands that in the interest of survival, nations will often engage in clandestine operations that involve unsavory characters and procedures. No democracy in history has ever refrained from engaging at times in such activities.

Many liberals will complain about Israel's role in the Iran-Contra affair, claiming that they hold Israel to a higher moral standard in the conduct of its foreign policy. If Israel, however, had always conducted its foreign policy according to utopian moral standards, it never would have survived its first forty years. For any student painfully aware of the realities of Middle East politics, Israel's involvement in the Iran-Contra affair is neither incomprehensible nor shameful.

Chapter 16
The Liberals and Soviet Jewry: The 1987 March On Washington

"President Reagan was right to call the Soviet Union the 'Evil Empire,' and he is also right to negotiate with them for a limitation on nuclear weapons."
—Edward I. Koch, Mayor of New York, at the December 6, 1987 March on Washington for Soviet Jewry

The liberal theology in the post-McGovern era of the Democratic Party has as one of its cornerstones the doctrine of "moral equivalence" between the United States of America and the Soviet Union. When moderates and conservatives express alarm about the Soviet buildup of offensive first-strike nuclear weapons, adherents of the "new liberalism" argue that the Soviets are merely reacting to our own defense expenditures. When human rights activists condemn the Soviet Union for human rights violations, the new liberals often will shrug their shoulders and say that after all, America has mistreated its ethnic minorities, including Blacks and Hispanics. When individuals voice their concern about Soviet beachheads in Cuba and Nicaragua, the new liberals will rationalize this totalitarian intrusion into the Western Hemisphere by stating that after all, the United States has troops and bases involved in NATO in Western Europe.

This doctrine of "moral equivalence" totally ignores the fundamental differences between the American way of life and that of the Soviet Union. The United States of America certainly is not a perfect Utopia; however, it has protected freedom of expression to an extent almost unparalleled in the history of civilization. While we have not always acted with perfect honor in international affairs, we have a record of magnanimity toward defeated foes (e.g. Germany, Japan, etc.) unprecedented in the annals of human existence.

By contrast, the Soviet Union represents the ultimate nightmare of the human experience. Joseph Stalin's butchery of Soviet peasants in moving toward his goal of total collectivization was surpassed only by Hitler's Holocaust. The Soviet Union has enslaved Eastern Europe under its totalitarian suzerainty and is presently conducting a war of genocide in Afghanistan.

Much to their credit, the "old liberals," such as Hubert Humphrey and Henry Jackson, never espoused the "moral equivalence" doctrine but instead were just as vehemently opposed to Soviet repression and expansionism as their conservative counterparts. Indeed, Ed Koch is loyal to the very best of the "old liberal" tradition of resistance to any further Soviet conquest and persecution. In spite of liberals like Connecticut Representative Sam Gejdenson who, as stated previously, mocked President Reagan for his use of the phrase "Evil Empire" in describing the Soviet Union, Ed Koch totally supported the usage of this phrase by the President. Unlike Gejdenson, Koch realized that the phrase was totally accurate for a nation which currently presents the greatest threat to world Jewry, both in its internal persecution of Jews and in its support for enemies of the Jewish people, such as the PLO, the Sandinistas in Nicaragua, and Syria.

The issue of Soviet Jewry poses a dilemma for modern liberalism. The rank and file of American Jewry has an all too vivid memory of Hitler's Holocaust and a sense of guilt that American Jewry did not take sufficient political action at that time. Therefore, American Jewry will be particularly sensitive and vigorous in combatting any perceived threats to the welfare of Soviet Jewry. Since conservatives are less equivocal than liberals as to the nature and practices of the Soviet government, the issue of Soviet Jewry presents an opportunity for conservatives to attract Jewish voters. Therefore, in order to avoid any risk of losing the allegiance of Jewish voters, liberal politicians at the time of the December, 1987 March on Washington for Soviet Jewry tended to abandon all vestiges of "moral equivalence" in denouncing Soviet persecution of Jewry.

I participated in the march on December 6, 1987. It was a day of deep emotion regarding our Jewish brethren in the Soviet Union that I personally will never forget. Yet even amidst this solidarity of American Jews of all political stripes, I could not help but notice two factors involving Jewish political behavior. The first was that the liberal posture on the issue had proven to be somewhat effective in blunting the appeal of conservative politicians who had long labored on behalf of Soviet Jewry. Second, in spite of the behavior of leading liberal politicians, there are significant elements among the Jewish liberal left who even now play down the threat to Soviet Jewry and remain firmly committed to the doctrine of "moral equivalence." Each of these topics merits separate consideration.

*   *   *   *   *

The March on Washington for Soviet Jewry on
Sunday, December 6, 1987 was occasioned by the visit
of Soviet Leader Mikhail Gorbachev to Washington to
sign the INF treaty. Over 250,000 American Jews
(approximately four percent of the entire American
Jewish population) attended the demonstration.

Also attending the demonstration were some of the
leading candidates for the Presidency in 1988. Vice
President George Bush, Senator Robert Dole, and
Representative Jack Kemp all gave speeches. Senator
Albert Gore circulated through the crowd greeting
various demonstrators. Numerous members of both
the House of Representatives and Senate from both
political parties were introduced from the rostrum,
and several gave speeches.

I found it highly significant that it was the liberal
members of Congress who received the loudest and
most fervent applause. This was an occasion where the
Soviet Union was being condemned for its domestic
and foreign policies. Yet the loudest applause from the
throng was often reserved for liberal Democrats advocating appeasement of the Soviets and imprudent cuts
in our defense budget, resulting in a weakening of our
posture vis-a-vis the Soviets. Among these applause
recipients were such liberals as Senator Ted Kennedy
of Massachusetts, Representative Barney Frank of
Massachusetts, and Representative Ted Weiss of
New York.

This applause reinforced my belief that many
American Jews reflexively believe that their true allies in the Congress are the liberals, regardless of how
counter-productive liberal policies may be on many

issues of Jewish concern, including that of Soviet
Jewry. It was not appeasement but rather American
strength and resolve which had brought Gorbachev in
the first place to the negotiating table where America
could express its concerns on human rights, particularly on the issue of Soviet Jewry. A key ingredient of
American resolve was the Strategic Defense Initiative
Program, labeled by the liberals as "Star Wars." Even
thoughtful liberals conceded that the determination of
the Reagan administration to pursue this program
was the key factor in Soviet willingness to negotiate
both a reduction of armaments and human rights
issues. As Morris B. Abram, Chairman of the Conference of Presidents of Major American Jewish Organizations and of the National Conference on Soviet
Jewry stated in an article in the Saturday,
December 5, 1987 issue of the *New York Times* entitled
"Why March in Washington for Soviet Jews," the
summit was "the first time that the Soviet Union has
ever explicitly agreed in advance that international
human rights are proper issues to be dealt with at a
summit conference." Even the liberal columnist Ken
Auletta conceded in his Sunday, December 27, 1987
column in the *New York Daily News* , "I hate admitting
it, but this dangerous illusion (Strategic Defense Initiative) helped lure the Soviets to the negotiating
table." In addition, Morris Abram credited the effort by
President Reagan, Secretary of State George P. Shultz
and Congress "to keep the (human rights) issue on the
agenda at all meetings with Soviet officials."

Ironically, Kennedy, Frank and Weiss all opposed
the Strategic Defense Initiative and were among the
most vitriolic critics of the Reagan administration, an
administration which openly supported the March

and pursued the policies mentioned above which resulted in the issue of Soviet Jewry finally getting on
the agenda at a summit conference. Yet these three
individuals were greeted by the crowd as heroes,
proving that many Jews believe that somehow liberalism has become the modern Torah of Israel.

This glorification of Messrs. Kennedy, Frank, and
Weiss becomes all the more ironic when one considers
that the most committed Representative in the Congress on Soviet Jewry, Jack Kemp, a conservative
Republican, received sparse, perfunctory applause
when introduced.

Even liberal Democrats have noted and com-
mended Jack Kemp for his concern on such Jewish
issues as the security and survival of the State of Israel
and the plight of Soviet Jewry. During the January
1988 Republican Presidential candidate debate in
which she served as moderator, Representative Patri-
cia Schroeder (D-Colorado), one of the most noteworthy liberals in the House of Representatives, com-
mended Kemp for his stand in these two areas. At the
Washington March itself, after Kemp has completed
his speech, he was hugged by Vladimir Slepak, the
famous Soviet Jewish dissident who last year was
finally permitted to emigrate to Israel.

Clearly, those most informed about the issue of
Soviet Jewry are aware of Jack Kemp's contribution to
the cause. There has been no small amount of press
coverage devoted to various measures he has sponsored in the House of Representatives to deny assistance to the Soviet Union unless it eases its policies on
Jewish emigration. In spite of this, and due to his
conservatism and identification as a Republican, his
efforts go largely unappreciated by the Jewish commu-

nity, while such liberals as Kennedy, Frank, and Weiss undeservedly get the applause. This indeed proves that the myth of Jewish and liberal convergence of interests dies hard.

As mentioned above, liberal politicians, concerned about losing the allegiance of Jewish voters, have refrained from rationalizing Soviet anti-Semitism or in any way downplaying its virulence. There are growing signs, however, that significant left liberal Jewish elements now feel free to downplay the extent of Soviet anti-Semitism while at the same time accusing the Reagan administration and the State of Israel of utilizing the issue of Soviet Jewry for their own political purposes.

One such organization is the New Jewish Agenda (NJA), an organization which has been praised by such leading liberals as the actor, Ed Asner, former U.S. Secretary of Commerce and International B'nai B'rith President, Philip M. Klutznick, and the lesbian-feminist writer, Adrienne Rich.

During the December, 1987 March on Washington on behalf of Soviet Jewry, I had the occasion to meet several representatives of the New Jewish Agenda. I understood that the organization had downplayed various reports of Sandinista anti-Semitism in Nicaragua; accordingly, I took advantage of the occasion to ask one of the New Jewish Agenda marchers what the organization's position was on Sandinista anti-Semitism. He responded by saying, "Well, you know there were only fifty Jews in Nicaragua."

I found this response interesting in view of the fact that I always believed that it was wrong to persecute even *one* Jew on account of his Jewish origin. I never knew that there was a numerical threshold of Jews below which a Marxist nation could persecute them with impunity.

More interesting to me, however, was a flyer distributed by the organization entitled "In Solidarity With Soviet Jewry; in Support of Détente and Disarmament."

The flyer conceded that anti-Semitism did exist in the Soviet Union, although it tended to understate its extent. For example, the flyer called upon the Soviet government to re-evaluate the denial of visas to some 11,.000 Jewish applicants. The New Jewish Agenda conceded that many denials were based on "spurious grounds." It is noteworthy, however, that this numerical estimate of 11,000 is ridiculously small. According to Morris Abram, "Contrary to publicity, glasnost has not applied to Russian Jews. New immigration regulations, passed under Gorbachev, are more restrictive than under Brezhnev. It will make it much more difficult for the *400,000* Jews who want to emigrate."

The NJA statement goes on to support the right of Soviet Jews to study and teach Hebrew. The NJA, however, shows unbelievable naiveté by its statement that "the recent passage of Soviet legislation on private employment, if implemented and actively enforced, should put an end to the prosecution of private Hebrew and Judaica teachers on charges of 'parasitism'." Implicit in this statement is the notion that legislation passed by phony Soviet legislative bodies is something more than a cover for their continuing anti-Semitic activities. The Soviets have had a continuing policy of anti-Semitism since the early 1950's, and one has to be incredibly ingenuous to believe that such legislation marks a new Soviet policy designed to eradicate anti-Semitism.

The real heart of this NJA flyer, however, is its twofold contention that: 1) Jewish leaders are over-playing the extent of Soviet anti-Semitism; and 2) any effort to link arms control and trade to Soviet conces-sions on Jewish emigration is immoral and a disaster for all concerned.

While the NJA acknowledges that Jewish life in the Soviet Union is not without its problems, it at-tempts to downplay the extent of Soviet anti-Semitism by stating, "We must begin by recognizing that, to date, even by the most liberal estimates, only a quarter of the Soviet Jewish population can be said to have expressed any interest in emigration." The statement goes on to say that "We believe that exaggerated claims of a Soviet Jewish Holocaust abuse the memory of those who perished at the hands of the Nazis and exacerbate tensions rather than promoting the goals of pluralism, peace, and open emigration."

These quotations constitute a hideous distortion of the issue. To say *"only* a quarter" of the Jewish popu-lation is interested in emigration is to imply that somehow this is a small percentage of the population. In any nation, however, where a quarter of any ethnic group desires to emigrate, one must conclude beyond any reasonable doubt that conditions of life for that ethnic population have become *totally* intolerable.

Furthermore, the NJA is attempting to insinuate that various advocates of Soviet Jewry are claiming that conditions for Soviet Jewry are equivalent to those in Nazi Germany. I have never, however, read any statement from even the most fervent Soviet Jewish advocate in which there are any claims that

Soviet Jewry is undergoing a physical "Holocaust." It is not much comfort to Soviet Jewry, however, that their living conditions are better than those of the Jews in Nazi Germany.

While downplaying Soviet Jewish persecution, the obvious goal of the NJA is to defeat attempts to link arms control and trade to emigration. The NJA labels such linkage as "disastrous" and states that "tension, confrontation and the threat of a nuclear holocaust do not serve Jewish—or any—interests. In fact, opportunities for emigration and Jewish self expression have been greatest during periods of improved relations."

Would the NJA suggest, however, that the Reagan administration sign arms control treaties with the Soviets and allow trade in technology and agriculture to continue unimpeded while Jews continue to suffer? What the NJA does not state is that, in the words of Morris Abram, "Glasnost has not made any fundamental difference for the two million Soviet Jews left behind" in spite of the NJA's glib assertion that a lessening of Soviet tensions with the West results automatically in improved conditions for Soviet Jews. In spite of a thaw in American-Soviet relations during 1987, the Soviets passed harsh regulations which, accordingly to Abram, "restrict the right to leave to cases of family reunification." Furthermore, Abram pointed out that Soviet authorities continue arbitrarily to invoke "state secrecy" laws. Soviet Jews remain as the only ethnic or religious group denied institutions to teach their language, religion and culture. Finally, as Abram points out, 1987 immigration figures for Soviet Jews are one-fifth of those of 1979. Is this the improvement in Jewish life that the NJA envisioned during détente?

The Soviet Union never has done anything out of altruistic concerns. If improvements are to be witnessed in the daily lives of Soviet Jews, it will only come about because the Soviet leadership is anxious to obtain arms control treaties, trade, and technology from the United States, and thus will make concessions to Soviet Jews in order to obtain these goals.

A good example of the effectiveness of linkage was the release during the past two years by the Soviet Union of Natan Sharansky and Vladimir Slepak. The Reagan administration had continuously insisted on the release of these two prisoners of conscience. The Soviets only released them when they realized that any further progress on trade and arms control with the Reagan administration would depend upon at least some small concession by the Soviets on Jewish emigration. Certainly, the Soviets did not release these refuseniks out of the goodness of their hearts.

The real targets of the NJA statement are, however, the Reagan administration itself and the present National Unity Coalition government in the State of Israel.

As to the Reagan administration, the statement contends "for the Reagan administration, our concern (on Soviet Jewry) is a tool to be used in recruiting American Jews to the 'Evil Empire' approach to U.S.-Soviet relations." As to the present government in Israel, Soviet Jews represent "potential Occupied Territories Settlers and a solution to Israel's skilled labor shortage...Soviet Jews have been used as pawns in the Cold War: they must not now become pawns for Israel's internal policy."

If there was ever a more clear example of McCarthyism of the Left, one can find it in these previous NJA statements. They imply that neither the Reagan administration nor the State of Israel has any real concern about the welfare of Soviet Jewry. The NJA totally disregards the effort of President Reagan, as mentioned above by Morris Abram, and those of George Shultz, who in fact visited a Jewish Seder in Moscow while on his April, 1987 visit. The NJA implies that Israel has no real concern with Soviet Jewish refugees except as pawns in their settlement policy. Perhaps the leaders of the NJA should attempt to tell this to Natan Sharansky, who was willing to undergo the tortures of the Gulag in order to finally achieve freedom as a Jew in the land he longed for, *Eretz Yisrael*. I am sure that Sharansky did not regard himself as some sort of Israeli pawn.

In fact, for me, the high point of the Washington demonstration was when Sharansky was introduced to the throng. We all began to sing *Am Yisrael Chai*— meaning "the nation of Israel lives." To me, Sharansky represents perhaps the greatest living Jew. To the NJA, I suppose, he is one of "only a quarter of the Soviet Jewish population" who have expressed any interest in emigration.

As mentioned above, the NJA has received critical acclaim in Jewish liberal circles. It is clear, however, that this organization is willing to sacrifice the fate of Soviet Jewry on the Golden Calf of Détente. I only hope and pray that the goals of the New Jewish Agenda do not soon become synonymous with the goals of the American Jewish liberal community.

Chapter 17
The Liberals, Israel and the Palestine Arabs: 1988

"Geographically Palestine is part of Syria; its indigenous inhabitants belong to the Syrian branch of the Arab family of nations; all their culture and tradition link them to the Arab peoples."
—Testimony of the Arab Office in Jerusalem before the Anglo-American Committee of Inquiry, March, 1946

"It is common knowledge that Palestine is nothing but Southern Syria."
—Ahmed Shukairy, the first Chief of the Palestine Liberation Organization, before the United Nations Security Council on May 31, 1956.

During the 1930's, as in the 1980's there existed a virtual political war between those individuals and institutions labeled as "liberal" and those labeled as "conservative." The liberals and their champion, Franklin Delano Roosevelt, controlled the Presidency, but their efforts were often thwarted by a conservative Supreme Court, a Congress often dominated by a coalition of conservative Republicans and southern Democrats, and a conservative press.

In the 1980's, however, it is now the conservatives, with their ideological champion in the person of President Reagan who control the Presidency, while the liberals now dominate the Congress and continue to heavily influence the opinions of the Supreme Court. Similarly, the conservative press of the 1930's has been totally transformed into the liberal media of the 1980's, populated in large part by individuals who were graduated from institutions of higher learning during the 1960's and 1970's when these institutions were largely populated by a liberal faculty and student body.

The new liberal alliance of the Congress, Judiciary, and the press has for the most part held together successfully, most notably in blocking the efforts of the Reagan administration to abrogate racial quotas, euphemistically labeled as "affirmative action." On the issue of the Israeli-Arab conflict, however, the liberal alliance has often foundered.

Since the Yom Kippur War of 1973, the media, erstwhile supporters of the Jewish State, has continuously expressed its increasing support and sympathy for Palestinian Arab aspirations. The Israelis, once described by the press as valiant underdogs, are now often portrayed as militaristic and insensitive to "the human rights of the Palestinian Arab people." It is Israel and not the Arabs, that the media often portrays as being the obstacle to a peaceful solution of all Middle East conflict issues. Anti-Israel sentiment among the American media reached its zenith during the 1982 Israeli invasion of Lebanon, when many American press reporters and television commentators excoriated Israel, most notably *Time* (which ultimately was found by the jury in the Ariel Sharon lawsuit to have wrongly accused him of responsibility for the massacre of Palestinians by Lebanese Christians in two Beirut refugee camps) and NBC television, most notably its former anchorman, John Chancellor, who during the height of the Lebanese conflict made references to "imperial Israel." Most recently, during the riots by Arab Palestinians in Gaza and the West Bank during December, 1987 and early 1988, the print, television, and radio media have almost universally portrayed the Israeli government as a repressive regime which discriminated against native Palestinian Arabs and created the conditions that led to a spontaneous uprising by Palestinian Arabs who thirsted for "self determination."

While the liberal dominated media has definitely tilted toward the Arabs, its fellow liberal ally, the Congress, has thus far resisted this trend and retained a basically pro-Israel orientation. This continuing liberal Congressional support for Israel is, in my view, simply attributable to one reason: fear of the Jewish vote. I make this contention about this motivation in view of the fact that liberal support of Israel in the Congress is totally inconsistent with the liberal isolationist stance on other foreign policy and defense issues.

On national defense, liberal members of Congress continuously vote to limit expenditures; yet they vote for increased military support of Israel, obviously to mollify their Jewish constituents. This support of Israel is not only inconsistent with the liberals' vote on our own defense budget; it is also inconsistent with their attitude about rendering assistance to other foreign governments. For example, liberals in Congress were at the forefront of opposition to the placement of various weapon systems in Europe, such as the Pershings and the neutron bomb.

In addition, liberal members of Congress tend to support appeasement and rapprochement with every third world Marxist-oriented revolutionary movement, including the Sandinistas in Nicaragua, the African National Congress in South Africa, the Communist Revolutionaries in El Salvador, and the Marxist regimes in Angola and Mozambique; yet for the most part, liberal members of Congress will not espouse a policy of appeasement and rapprochement with the Palestine Liberation Organization (PLO).

It is my firm belief that if liberal members of Congress did not fear Jewish electoral reaction, they would join their liberal allies in the press in displaying increased support and sympathy for the PLO.

There are two factors, however, which could result in liberal political figures perceiving a decreased potency in American Jewish reaction against support for the PLO.

The first would be the abolition of the electoral college as the method for electing the President. Under the electoral college system, the candidate capturing a plurality of the state's votes captures all the state's electoral votes. The Jewish vote is a key factor in such crucial states as California, New York, Massachusetts, New Jersey and Florida; thus any liberal member of Congress contemplating a Presidential campaign must avoid antagonizing Jewish voters or risk losing the electoral votes of these key states. If the electoral college were abolished, however, and if Presidents were elected by direct popular vote, a liberal candidate for President could afford to lose the Jewish vote in these aforementioned key states and simply compensate by picking up gentile votes in other states. There is little doubt that abolition of the electoral college would emasculate the Jewish vote as a critical factor in Presidential elections. Fortunately, such an abolition does not appear on the horizon; therefore, liberal politicians still must respect Jewish concerns about Israel.

The second factor would be the development of a liberal Jewish consensus for appeasement of the implacable Arab foes of Israel. Ominously, such a liberal Jewish ideological trend appeared in early 1988, as various significant Jewish liberals reacted to Palestinian violence in Gaza and the West Bank as if Israeli intransigence were the cause. The Tuesday, December 22, 1987 edition of the *New York Times* reported such Jewish liberal reaction.

The *Times* reported that Rabbi Alexander M. Schindler, President of the Reform Jewish Union of American Hebrew Congregations, stated that the violence should "shock Israel's Government" into aggressively negotiating an end to the Israeli occupation of former Arab territory. The *Times* quoted Schindler as stating "Israel simply cannot sit in the territories and wait for peace to come...The status quo sows the seed of endless conflict."

Echoing Rabbi Schindler's sentiments was a group of thirty prominent Jews promulgating a statement under the name of "American Committee for Israel Peace Center." The *Times* reported the statement as saying that the recent violence left the signers "anxious and concerned." The statement then asserted that the "present situation in the occupied territories illustrates more clearly than ever the urgent need to embark upon peace negotiations."

Two noted luminaries of the left liberal Jewish community signed the statement, to wit, Letty Cottin Pogrebin, an editor at Ms. Magazine and Rabbi Balfour Brickner, of whom I spoke in Chapter 4.

Never has there been a more misdirected statement than that of the liberal heroes of the American Committee for Israel Peace Center. For over twenty

years since the end of the June 1967 war, Israel has not
only been willing but in fact *eager* to negotiate with the
Arab states the status of the territories Israel won in
a war to prevent a second holocaust of the Jewish
people. The only state to take Israel up on this offer
was Egypt, who has received from Israel *all* Egyptian
territory Israel had captured in the June 1967 war.
This is hardly the act of an intransigent Israeli government. Contrary to the allegation of Schindler, Israel
has not simply been waiting for peace to come; she has
in fact, been inviting a simple phone call for over
twenty years from those who are contentedly waiting
for Israel to weaken and vanish in a war.

No, despite the contentions of Schindler, et al., the
status quo remains because the Arab states continue
to desire the destruction of the Jewish state and refuse
to recognize its existence. They have failed four times
on the battlefield; now, they place their hopes in
wooing support for Palestinian Arab nationalism, a
convenient camouflage for Israel's destruction. Indeed, this camouflage becomes all the more evident
when one examines the history of the Arab-Israeli
conflict.

Zionism was not a simple movement to form a
Jewish State as a result of a romantic desire to return
to the ancient homeland. Instead, a Jewish State was
an absolute necessity to enable Jewry to have a safe
haven where they could determine their own destiny
in a world which had proven to be a charnel house for
the Jewish people.

But did Jewry constitute a nation? The answer is a
resounding *yes*. In political science, a nation is defined
as a people who view themselves as having a common
past and a common future aspiration. When a Jew

reads his Siddur or Passover Haggadah, he recalls his common past with world Jewry, including the Exodus of the Jewish people from Egypt, the original migration to *Eretz Yisrael*, the building of the Temple, and the exile from the ancient homeland. The world may resent the survival of the Jewish people as a national entity, but survive we have.

The Israel-Arab conflict results from the fact that when the Zionists attempted to lead the Jewish people to their ancient homeland, it was already occupied by another people, the Arabs. The Jews were not the first people to attempt to form a nation in a location currently occupied by others; the United States of America, for example, was founded by Englishmen migrating to a land already occupied by the American Indians; England was founded by Anglos and Saxons who drove out the native Celts. As the late eminent Jewish historian Jacob Talmon stated, "The chilling fact (is) that there has not been a nation in history, including the mightiest powers and richest civilizations on earth which has not established itself through invading, subjugating, expelling, or indeed annihilating vast native populations."

Every single significant Zionist faction, including both Labor and Revisionist, hoped that the Palestinian Arabs would agree to live peacefully within a Jewish State. Indeed, the founder of Zionism, Theodore Herzl, stated his hope in his book, *Altneuland*, that the Arabs would react to the establishment of a Jewish State with the expression, "It was a blessing for all of us!"

The Zionists were not naive. They realized that the Arabs living in Palestine would resent living in a state with a Jewish majority and government. The most

accurate response to this, however, was given by Vla-
dimar Ze'ev Jabotinsky, who stated the following in a
speech before the British House of Lords on February
11, 1937:

> I have the profoundest feeling for the
> Arab case, insofar as that Arab case is not
> exaggerated... We maintain unanimously
> that the economic position of the Palestin-
> ian Arabs, under the Jewish colonization
> and owing to the Jewish colonization, has
> become the object of envy in all the sur-
> rounding countries, *so that the Arabs from
> those countries show clear tendency to
> immigrate into Palestine*. I have also
> shown to you already, that, in our
> submission, *there is no question of ousting
> the Arabs*. On the contrary, the idea is that
> Palestine, on both sides of the Jordan
> *should hold the Arabs, their progeny, and
> many millions of Jews*. What I do not deny
> is that in the process the Arabs of Pales-
> tine will necessarily become a minority in
> the country of Palestine. What I do deny is
> that *that* is a hardship. It is not a hardship
> on any race, any nation possessing so
> many National States now and so many
> more National States in the future. One
> fraction, one branch of that race, and not a
> big one, will have to live in someone else's
> State: well that is the case with all the
> mightiest nations of the world...It is quite
> understandable that the Arabs of Pales-
> tine would also prefer Palestine to be the
> Arab State Number 4, Number 5, or

Number 6—that I quite understand: *But when the Arab claim is confronted with our Jewish demand to be saved, it is like the claims of appetite versus the claims of starvation.*

Who could deny the justice in Jabotinsky's statement? The great mass of the Arab people would live in independent Arab States, and only that portion of the Arab people living in Palestine would live under foreign domination. Is it unjust for the Jewish people to ask for a single small state in a world where the Arabs have twenty states?

Furthermore, as shown by the quotations at the beginning of this Chapter, there is a significant question as to whether the Palestinian Arabs, per se, constitute a separate nation. There is no difference in the culture, religion or physical appearance of Palestinian Arabs from any Arabs living in any other geographic location in the Middle East. Throughout world history, there never has been a separate Palestine Arab State; indeed, until after the June, 1967 war, Palestinian Arabs always maintained that they were no different ethnically from any other Arabs and that in fact Palestine was nothing more than Southern Syria. The Palestinian Arabs prior to 1948 never thought of themselves as having any different history from that of their fellow Arabs. As for those Palestinians who became refugees as a result of the 1947–1948 Arab-Israeli war, they were now living in Arab lands which had a culture no different from that of the Arabs from Palestine.

The Zionists hoped to establish their State without the violent normal birth of nations described by Jacob Talmon above. Unfortunately, the Palestinian Arabs refused to acquiesce to a Jewish State even in the small portion of Palestine granted to the Jews by the United Nations Partition Resolution passed in November, 1947.

It was the Palestinian Arabs, supported by their neighboring Arab States, who started the 1947–1948 war against the establishment of the State of Israel; the Jews counter-attacked against the Arabs and won. It was a result of this counter-attack that so many Palestinian Arabs became refugees. Thus, the Palestinian Arabs became refugees *as a result of a war which they started.*

It is very interesting to note that the November, 1947 United Nations resolution called for the establishment of a separate, independent Palestinian Arab state. Only one party in the Middle East supported the establishment of this Palestinian Arab state: the *Zionists! Every single Arab State opposed the United Nations resolution which would have created an independent Palestine Arab State.*

The Palestinian Arabs were not primarily concerned with whether Palestine was a separate Arab country or part of a larger Pan-Arabic Union. Their sole concern was that not one inch of Palestine should be controlled by a Jewish State. As a result of the 1947–1948 war, the major portion of Palestine not conquered by the Jews was annexed by Jordan,. It is interesting to note that during the years 1948 to the June, 1967 war when Gaza was ruled by Egypt and the West Bank was ruled by Jordan, the Palestinian Liberation Organization never demanded that these remaining Arab portions of Palestine form an independent Palestine State. Contrary to all the nonsense currently written about the Palestinians seeking self-determination, they simply wanted Israel, and they wanted all of it. Had they simply sought self-determination in an Arab Palestinian State and been willing to live side by side with a Jewish State, they could have achieved this goal.

Instead, the PLO sponsored terrorist raids in the middle of the night that resulted in the slaughter of Jewish men, women, and children living in various *kibbutzim* and *moshavim*. This cycle of Palestinian terror and Israeli reprisal ultimately led to the June, 1967 war and the Israeli conquest of all of ancient Palestine west of the Jordan River. The Yom Kippur War of 1973 confirmed that Israel was here to stay.

It is interesting to note that despite all these Jewish victories, the PLO has never renounced its goal of ultimately destroying the Jewish State. The Yasser Arafats, et als., however, have become masters of public relations. While not renouncing their goal of annihilation of the Jewish State, they now soft pedal this goal and insist that all they are seeking is self determination.

But if this is the case, however, why didn't the Palestinians simply seek self determination in Palestine when they could have achieved it during the years 1948 through 1967, when much of Palestine was still in Arab hands. Is it any wonder that Israel should regard this expressed Palestinian desire for "self determination" in Palestine as simply a camouflage for the eventual destruction of the Jewish State? Is it little wonder that Israeli leaders should consider "Palestinian Arab Nationalism" to be counterfeit when the Palestinian Arabs themselves always expressed the view that they were not a separate and distinct people from the rest of the entire Arab people per se? The Arab people as a whole could justifiably claim to be one nation since they have one common historical memory.

The Palestinian Arabs could no more claim to be a separate nation than could New Yorkers or Mexican Americans.

Israel captured the West Bank and Gaza in a war for its survival started by its Arab adversaries in 1967. Having captured these territories in a war of self defense, Israel has every right to keep them.

In my view, however, it is not in Israel's best interest to keep these territories, since the high Arab birth rate could result in the Jews becoming a minority in the country, accordingly resulting through election in the end of the Jewish State. Thus, it is in Israel's best interest to return the territories to Arab control, subject to adjustments of the borders for security reasons and the retention of all Jerusalem by Israel. If the Jordanians, led by King Hussein, are willing to negotiate, then Israel could make a deal resulting in the redelivery of the West Bank to Jordanian control. Under no circumstance, however, will Israel turn over control of the West Bank to enemies like Arafat who have sought to destroy the Jewish state.

Suicide is one of the most heinous crimes in Judaism, and the Israelis are not about to commit it by delivery of the West Bank into the hands of the PLO. In spite of the foolish sentiments expressed by liberals such as Schindler, Brickner, and Pogrebin, it is not Israel who has been intransigent, but rather all the Arab States, except Egypt, who have refused to meet with Israel in face to face negotiations. In the words of the late Israeli Prime Minister, Golda Meir, Israel is not about to die so that it may be loved by the world. Unlike the liberals of the United States, the leaders of Israel know that to let down one's guard in the face of an implacable enemy is merely an invitation to another ultimate holocaust.

Conclusion: Toward A New Covenant

When I informed my friends that I was writing this book, their immediate reaction was, in most cases, "Why are you writing a book specifically geared to Jews and their voting attitudes? Is there any reason why Jews should have any significantly different political attitude than anyone else?"

Ideally, I would agree with my friends. As I stated in the introduction to this book, the best interests of the American Jewish community are identical to the best interests of the American community at large. If Jewish voting attitudes simply mirrored the American public at large, then there would be no raison d'être for this book.

The fact of the matter, however, is that Jews *have* had voting patterns that are significantly at variance with those of the general American public. That in itself would not concern me, except for the fact that American Jewish liberal politicians have attempted to make liberalism part of Jewish theology, similar to the centrality of the Torah and Talmud in Jewish philosophy.

This, more than anything else, is the reason for this book. As I have stated throughout, the liberal theology is not only at variance with the general attitude of the American public at large; it is also most deleterious to the welfare of the Jewish community. That is why I will continue to scream from the rooftops that the covenant between the American Jewish community and American liberalism must finally be severed.

This covenant is of significantly long duration,

originating in the New Deal years of the 1930's. While I disputed the tenets of the old liberalism, I would not have been sufficiently alarmed by it to write this book. Certainly, while I disagreed with the Harry Trumans and the Hubert Humphreys, these were high-minded men who in many ways left our country a better place for centuries to come. What *has* alarmed me, however, and what most Jews have failed to recognize is that the definition and principles of American liberalism have significantly changed. In the years of Harry Truman, liberalism meant strong anti-Communism and resistance to Soviet aggression. Today, it means Blame America First. Prior to the 1960's, liberalism meant equality of opportunity; today's liberalism, however, worships equality of result in the form of quotas and affirmative action. The old liberalism advocated a safety net for those who could not help themselves; today's liberalism, however, promotes cradle-to-grave welfare protection.

The old liberalism fought anti-Semitism in all forms; today's liberalism seeks to temporize with the Jesse Jacksons and the Louis Farakkhans.

The old liberalism followed the tradition of Harry Truman and John F. Kennedy in being willing to furnish military assistance to allies of shared values throughout the globe; the new liberalism is formed on the isolationist tradition of a Hamilton Fish.

Thus, as mentioned previously, Jews continue to be the loyal bride to the liberal groom; however, the liberal groom has changed radically, and it is time for a divorce.

Yet as we enter into the presidential campaign year of 1988, there are signs that the loyal Jewish bride is incredibly masochistic and unwilling to consider

even the possibility of divorce. A few items will suffice:
1) Ann F. Lewis, a Jewess and a sister of Representative Barney Frank (D-Mass.) is serving as a campaign consultant to the Reverend Jesse Jackson, perhaps the most anti-Semitic candidate for President in this century! 2) Rabbi Alexander Schindler, the leader of the Union of American Hebrew Congregations, the leading organization of Reform Judaism in America, stated on nationally televised news reports during January, 1988 that Israeli policy in Gaza of physically beating Arab perpetrators of violence was contrary to Jewish ethics. Yet while Rabbi Schindler was castigating his own people, he failed to note that by Middle Eastern standards, Israel was a paragon of morality in dealing with domestic uprisings! Doesn't Rabbi Schindler know about the slaughter of 5,000 people by the Syrian government in the city of Hom? Doesn't he know that in Judaism, if somebody comes to kill you, you are supposed to kill him first? Finally, as noted by New York City Council President Andrew Stein (himself a liberal with whom I often disagree), in the *New York Post* on January 25, 1988, Israel certainly has treated its Arab rioters with far more restraint than American police forces treated blacks in urban ghetto riots during the 1960's.

I have written a book dedicated to the proposition that liberalism is antithetical to Judaism and Jewish interests, and in 1988, I feel compelled to demonstrate that political masochism on the part of the Lewises and Schindlers of this world is certainly not ordained in the Torah.

I do not expect that readers of this book will rush out and wholeheartedly embrace the dogma of American conservatism. I do hope, however, that thoughtful

Jews will open their hearts and minds and realize that Jews must stop thinking automatically of the liberal credo as part and parcel of the Jewish law and way of life.

The 1988 presidential election will be a critical one for American Jews. Despite the passage of time, Jews are hardly at a stage in America where they can be totally sanguine about the future. History has shown that in declining economic times, Jews are usually the first scapegoats and victims. There are ominous signs on the horizon for Jews. The growth of black anti-Semitism has been frightening. There continues to be numerous incidents of anti-Semitic vandalism in areas of substantial Jewish concentration. Finally, there have been victories in local elections by the crazy anti-Semitic fringe party of Lyndon LaRouche.

It is not inconceivable that if we should at any point enter a severe economic recession, Jews would be the victim and scapegoat of a coalition of angry poor whites and blacks and the bizarre extremist fringe groups in the American body politic. Yet it is absolutely incredible that liberal Jews have failed to perceive this danger but have instead developed an obsession with the Jerry Falwells, who have absolutely no anti-Semitic designs whatsoever.

Despite all the myths of Jewish economic power, the only real power Jews have in our society is the ballot. Jews do tend to vote in numbers disproportionate to their societal percentage. Until the late 1970's, liberal politicians took the Jewish vote for granted. Now, there are signs that, in the words of Bobby Dylan, the times they are a-changin'.

As mentioned earlier in this book, Jewish voters continue to have an incomprehensible loyalty toward the Democratic party and liberal candidates in particular. However, there have been deviations from this model. While Ronald Reagan trailed both Carter and Mondale among Jewish voters in both his elections, he did pull significantly higher totals than did Republican candidates in the 1950's and 1960's. Even more significant, however, has been the emergence of a class of Jewish conservative intellectuals both in academia and in government. Among such individuals are Norman Podhoretz, the editor of *Commentary* magazine, Under-Secretary of State Elliot Abrams, theater critic Benjamin Stein, the writer Irving Kristol, and many others. These individuals, many of whom are former radicals and liberals, are beginning to have an impact among Jews which may hopefully result in a change of direction.

Such a change of direction is sorely needed if both American Jewry and the State of Israel are to have any real security in a world fraught with peril. If there is anything that the Bible teaches us, it is that Israel suffered the most when it worshipped false gods. Today, American Jewish conservatives feel that they must act in the prophetic tradition of an Hosea, Isaiah, and Jeremiah and implore American Jewry to turn away from the false god of liberalism.

Just as Judaism implores our people not to worship false gods, it also teaches us to have a convenant, a *brith* with our own sacred values. The political conservatism of American society today fully coincides with the Jewish values of justice, fairness, respect for the dignity of man, and the punishment of those forces of evil who would seek to destroy us. That is why the time is right for American Jewry to enter into a new covenant, a covenant with political conservatism.

Postscript: Election 1988

As this book went to press, Michael Dukakis and George Bush had emerged as the nominees of the Democratic and Republican parties, respectively. At a time when the American public has displayed a great deal of political volatility, it would be foolish for me to offer a prediction on the general election outcome. As far as the American Jewish community is concerned, however, the events of the 1988 nomination process, particularly the New York Democratic primary, have already confirmed my analysis of liberalism and the Jewish community in two ominous respects:

1. During the New York primary, Michael Dukakis specifically refused to rule out the possibility of the creation of a Palestinian Arab State on the West Bank and in Gaza. The overwhelming consensus of Israeli political leaders, both Labor and Likud, is that the Palestine Liberation Organization would certainly emerge as the political leadership of such a state and that the result would be a significant threat to Israeli security. Yet despite his detrimental position on the issue, Dukakis received in the New York primary a higher percentage of support from the Jewish community than almost any other ethnic group, getting 77 percent of their votes. Indeed, it was the New York primary that sealed the nomination for Dukakis, and the Jews may be said to have cast the decisive vote. The result is that by giving their blessing to a candidate who has already stated positions contrary to the best interests of the State of Israel, the Jews have lost all leverage within the Democratic Party. American

Jewry has given the Democratic Party leadership the clear and unmistakable signal that not even such positions as those taken by Dukakis will cause the majority of American Jewish voters to even hint that they will defect to the Republican Party.

2. During the New York Democratic primary, New York City Mayor Edward I. Koch courageously stated the obvious concerning Jesse Jackson: "He thinks maybe Jews and other supporters of Israel should vote for him - they have got to be crazy! In the same way they'd be crazy if they were Black and voted for someone who was praising Botha and the racist supporters of the South African Administration..." Jewish liberals pounced upon Koch, accusing him of exacerbating the divisions between the Jewish and the Black communities. The message is clear: If a left wing candidate is Black, he is immunized from condemnation for taking even the most outrageous anti-Jewish positions, as Jackson has throughout his political career.

These two developments in Campaign 1988 certainly did not surprise me, as they totally confirmed my earlier analysis of 1) Israel and the liberals and 2) the Democrats and Black anti-Semitism. As one examines the underlying facts behind these two developments, however, I despair more than ever that the overwhelming mass of American Jewish voters may not, before it is too late, realize that liberalism is a cancer that is eating away at the health and future of the American Jewish body politic.

*   *   *   *   *

On Tuesday, April 12, 1988, one week before the New York primary, Michael Dukakis appeared before the Conference of Presidents of Major American Jewish Organizations and gave his views on the Israeli-Arab conflict. While blaming Arab leaders for the unrest on the West Bank and Gaza, Dukakis refused to take a position ruling out the creation of a Palestinian Arab state. Dukakis said, "It is Israel, Jordan, Egypt and the Palestinian leaders who have to make these decisions. It's the parties themselves to the negotiations who have to make those judgments." Furthermore, unlike Tennessee Senator Albert Gore, Jr., who had previously appeared before the Conference and voiced "dismay" at Jesse Jackson's embrace of PLO leader Yasser Arafat, Dukakis refused to criticize Jackson or respond to a questioner's charge that Jackson is "an anti-Semite" and "a racist in reverse".

On that same date, Dukakis appeared before a group of *New York Daily News* writers and editors and displayed a frightening degree of ignorance of Middle East politics for a major political candidate. He stated that Israel was willing to negotiate with the PLO if it recognized Israel's right to exist, despite the statements of Israeli Prime Minister Yitzhak Shamir that Israel would not negotiate with the PLO under any circumstances.

Yet despite these positions and the presence on the ballot of Senator Gore, who throughout his Senate career vigorously championed the Israeli cause, New York Jewish Democrat voters, as stated earlier, gave 77 percent of their ballots to Dukakis, while giving Gore only 15 percent and Jackson 8 percent. One explanation for the failure of Gore to receive a higher percentage was that many Jewish voters feared a Jackson victory above all and felt that a vote for Gore would only serve to decrease Dukakis's percentage and thus result in a Jackson victory. There is some truth in that analysis. Nevertheless, by supporting Dukakis in spite of his positions on a Palestinian state, New York Jewish Democratic voters gave Dukakis the unmistakable signal that he could take their support for granted, despite what problems a Dukakis Administration may portend for the future security of the State of Israel.

Perhaps a more disturbing yet plausible explanation of the support Dukakis received from the Jewish community, in spite of his positions on Israel, is that the overwhelming majority of Jewish voters are less concerned than ever about particularly "Jewish issues." A good analysis of the Jewish body politic 1988 was made by Douglas Schoen, a political consultant, who was quoted in an article by James M. Perry in *The Wall Street Journal* on Friday, April 15, 1988. Mr. Schoen divides the Jewish vote into three groups: 1) the "ultra- orthodox rejectionists" Jews, who align themselves with the policies of the Shamir government; 2) "modern orthodox" Jews, who wear yarmulkes and "lead consciously Jewish community-oriented lives" who support with more restrained passion the Shamir government; and 3) the bulk of the Jewish vote, which consists of "people who lead much more assimilated lives, don't wear yarmulkes and don't go to religious services very often." According to Mr. Schoen, the first two groups only constitute 15 percent of the Jewish vote.

I believe that there is a great deal of validity in the Schoen analysis. It must be stated that the 85 percent of the Jewish community which Mr. Schoen places in the third group does contain many committed Conservative and Reform Jews, as well as committed yet strictly secular Jews, who are all very concerned about the welfare of the Jewish community as a collective group. Unfortunately, this third group also contains many individuals who are not concerned with the welfare of their fellow Jews, be they in Israel, the Soviet Union, or the United States. Many of these individuals vote the liberal line due to their adherence to the old myth that their status as an individual Jew might be threatened by conservative American politicians who would discriminate against Jews. Such voters, however, by and large, are not terribly concerned about the welfare of the State of Israel, although they may support it in a distant emotional way.

The 1988 Presidential campaign, more than ever, will display just how concerned Jewish voters are regarding the State of Israel. Never has the American Jewish electorate had a clearer choice. In direct contrast to Michael Dukakis, George Bush has publicly opposed the creation of a Palestinian Arab state on the West Bank and Gaza. When pressed by a *Newsday* reporter for further comment as to how he felt about the creation of such a state, he stated, "Nonsense! I know enough about the Middle East to know that if the Arabs are given a Palestinian State, even that will not bring peace to the Middle East...It's totally unacceptable to Israel and there are a lot of other countries over there that don't want that concept...The security and freedom of Israel are fundamental to both American strength and Middle East stability. Of equal importance is our moral obligation to the people of Israel. This does not mean we must adopt all of Israel's positions with respect to her ongoing debate with the Arab world. It does mean, simply put, that Israel must be able to count on American political and economic support and military assistance."

One should not be surprised with Bush's position. Bush served as Vice President in the most pro-Israel

administration in American history. Two days after
the New York primary in which Dukakis refused to
rule out the establishment of a Palestinian state, the
United States and Israel signed a new strategic agreement codifying and formalizing cooperation on a range
of military, economic, political and intelligence
matters. *The New York Times*, on Friday, April 22,
1988, describes this agreement as one long sought by
Israel as a public symbol of American commitment,
codifying "existing informal working arrangements
that have grown during the Reagan Administration."

Given the stark contrast between Bush and
Dukakis on the issue of Israel, one could only conclude
that if Dukakis still carries a great majority of the
Jewish vote, the majority of American Jews are either:
1) less concerned about Israel in making a choice for
President; or 2) wedded to the concept of liberalism to
such an extent so as to literally ignore policies pursued
by liberal candidates that are detrimental to both
Israel and the American Jewish community. Indeed, if
Dukakis so carries the Jewish vote, the Democrats
may feel totally secure in taking the Jewish vote for
granted for the foreseeable future. In short, the Jewish
community will have totally lost its leverage within
the Democratic Party, without compensating for this
loss by increasing participation and influence in the
Republican Party. This does not bode well for the
Jewish political future in America.

*   *   *   *   *

Ed Koch's assessment of Jews who would support
Jackson as "crazy" was 100 percent accurate. Far from
being a "racist" criticism, Koch's assessment of
Jackson was the same as the Mayor would have made

of any candidate who took such extremely anti-Semitic and anti-Israel positions. Only a racist in reverse could contend that Jackson's skin color immunized him from such criticism.

Yet Koch was villified to an extent that even he could not have foreseen. In a shameful display of political demagoguery, Mark Green, a prominent liberal activist and the Democrat candidate for the U.S. Senate in 1986, stated that Koch's comments about Jackson came "close to outright bigotry...Who is he to speak for all the Jews?" It is interesting, however, to note that Green never questioned the authority of Jesse Jackson to speak for all blacks. To smear Koch, however, as a bigot was pure and simple McCarthyism of the Left on the part of Mark Green.

Even more vitriolic, although certainly not unexpected, were the comments of Rabbi Balfour Brickner. He stated, "The mayor is again shooting from the hip...The Jewish community of New York City is perfectly capable of making up its mind about Jesse Jackson without the guidance of the mayor...(Koch) has also further exacerbated tensions, the already existing tensions between blacks and Jews in this City." On Tuesday, April 12, 1988, The *New York Times* further reported that Mr. Jackson had made "at least one Jewish convert" at a breakfast of business leaders at the Sheraton Centre on Monday, April 11, 1988, Brickner himself. The Times quoted Brickner as stating, "I wanted to know whether or not Jesse Jackson is a viable, credible candidate, and he is. What he says makes sense. I was persuaded."

Truly Rabbi Brickner has now distinguished himself, first by exonerating the Sandinistas from the charge of anti-Semitism, and next by defending and supporting Jesse Jackson. First, Brickner defends the

most anti-Semitic regime in the history of the Western
Hemisphere (even more anti-Semitic than the Peron
regime in Argentina in the 1950's) and next he exoner-
ates the most anti-Semitic major party candidate for
President in the twentieth century.

The political behavior of the Balfour Brickners and
the remaining percent of the Jewish electorate who
voted for Jackson in the New York primary is certainly
deleterious to the welfare of the Jewish community in
America; yet it is hardly a unique phenomenon in
Jewish history. There has always been a minority
group of Jews in any society who are willing to believe
the very best about enemies of the Jewish community,
as long as such enemies shared their particular ideology. In an excellent monograph published by Americans for a Safe Israel entitled "The Anti-New Jewish
Agenda," Rael Jean Isaac points out that even in
Weimar Germany, there was a small Jewish fringe
group called the National deutschen Juden which
actually identified with the emerging Nazi Party. This
group, led by Max Naumann, believed the Nazi leaders
to be "noble idealists". Isaac further describes the
ideology of the group:

"Naumann called on German Jews to bear with
their 'error' (anti-Semitism) and to understand the
true value of their thoughts and methods in the national struggle 'even if they behave as if they are our
enemies.' Once the Nazis came to power, the National
deutschen Juden were convinced that the noble ideas
would be realized and the anti-Semitism would 'fall
away.' "

Germany had its National deutschen Juden.
American Jewry has its Balfour Brickners and Ann
Lewises. Indeed, in the words of Ecclesiastes, there is
nothing new under the sun. While the National

deutschen Juden never received substantial publicity, however, the Balfour Brickners and Ann Lewises have the benefit of the media in their attempts to immunize Jackson from criticism. This undercuts the efforts of Jews to combat anti- Semitism on the part of all political leaders, be they White or Black.

In this context, I stress the word "leaders" because I am convinced that the overwhelming masses of the Black rank and file are not anti-Semitic. The Louis Farrakhans and Jesse Jacksons do appeal to anti-Semitic trends in the Black community. I believe such trends to be minority trends, however, and I do not regard the large Black vote received by Jackson as either a mandate for his programs within the Black community or as evidence of increased Black anti-Semitism. Instead, I regard his overwhelming percentage of the Black vote simply as the natural inclination of Blacks, as with any people (excluding the Jews, as I noted in Chapter 10), to vote for "one of their own." It is long overdue for a black man to be considered for President of the United States. It is, however, an historical tragedy that the first such Black was one who had a blatant anti-Semitic appeal and whose views were not representative of the Black rank and file.

Indeed, I am convinced that not only Jackson but Black leaders as a whole with the laudable exception of Roy Innis, the national chairman of the Congress of Racial Equality (CORE), maintain positions which are totally out of tune with the majority of the Black population. As noted by *The Correspondent*, the newspaper of CORE, various polls conducted by *The New York Times*, CBS and the Center for Media and Public Affairs placed most black leaders well to the left of rank and file Blacks on most social and political issues.

As examples, *The Correspondent* cited the following:

"Politics: 68 percent of the leaders call themselves liberals, compared to only 27 percent of all Black people."

"Affirmative Action: 77 percent of the leaders favor minority preferences in hiring and college placement, while 77 percent of all Blacks oppose them."

"Busing: 68 percent of the leaders favor busing compared to 47 percent of all blacks."

" 'Gay Rights': Three out of five Blacks oppose letting homosexuals teach in public schools; three in five leaders favor it."

"Abortion: 43 percent of Blacks favor a ban on all abortions, compared to only 14 percent of the leaders."

"Thirty percent of all Blacks approved of President Reagan's performance compared to 13 percent of the leaders."

How is it then that Black America today has a leadership whose views are so out of touch with the rank and file?

Much of the answer, I believe, lies in the fact that the Democratic Party has basically preempted the field of Black politics. The Republican Party has for too long refrained from any real effort to organize and expand its base in the Black community, thus allowing the Democrats virtual suzerainty of the Black electorate. As long as the Democratic Party controls the political pulse of the Black community, it will make every effort to increase the political power of left wing Blacks while attempting to squelch the aspirations of Black conservatives. Left wing leaders of Black organizations find that they have willing partners in the Democratic Party to assist them in maintaining hegemony over Black political life. An outstanding Black conservative, such as Roy Innis, is unable to call upon any significant corresponding assistance from the Republican Party within the Black community since the Republicans have basically relinquished the field of Black politics to the Democrats. I am not saying that Republicans have treated the Black community unfairly; I am saying that when Republican office holders have dealt effectively with problems facing the Black community, they have usually done so due to their own political ideology and not due to any real expectation that they can expand their base of support within the Black community.

Like the Jews, the Blacks are also victims of one party rule. As I stated in Chapter 2 and in Chapter 6, Jews and Blacks should share a common agenda of advocating free market economics as the key to economic progress for both communities. Such common cause, however, will only be made possible when both Jews and Blacks liberate themselves from the shackles of one political party domination. When this happens, Jews and Blacks will both find that their support will not be taken for granted by either political party and that they will obtain increased economic and political leverage in America as never before. This election year of 1988 is as good a year as any for both Blacks and Jews to begin this march together to political and economic liberation from the false god of liberalism.

Acknowledgements

This book was written during a time of very substantial change in both my personal and professional
life. I was very fortunate to have friends who have
sustained me through the highs and lows of the last
five years.

Particularly, I must thank Jerry and Gloria Baer,
Woody and Brenda Pollock, Mike and Lynda Ritter-
man, Ralph Villeca, Ira and Deborah Krauss, Jim
Madonna, Jennifer Monson and David Moll for always
being there when I needed encouragement and
guidance.

To Dominick Spadea, Olivia Fanelle, Tom Brui-
nooge, John Rocco, and Jeff Land, I offer thanks for
proving that political involvement can reward you
with life long friendships which make the heartaches
of political life all worthwhile.

To Jean Murphy and Mary Shevlin, my secretar-
ies, thanks for being my friends and sounding boards
and the unknown soldiers of this book.

And finally, once again I must thank Cantor Mordecai Fuchs for being the best brother a man could
have and to Neil for being all I could ask for in a son.

LUIS